M551 Sheridan

Written by Chris Hughes

Walk Around®

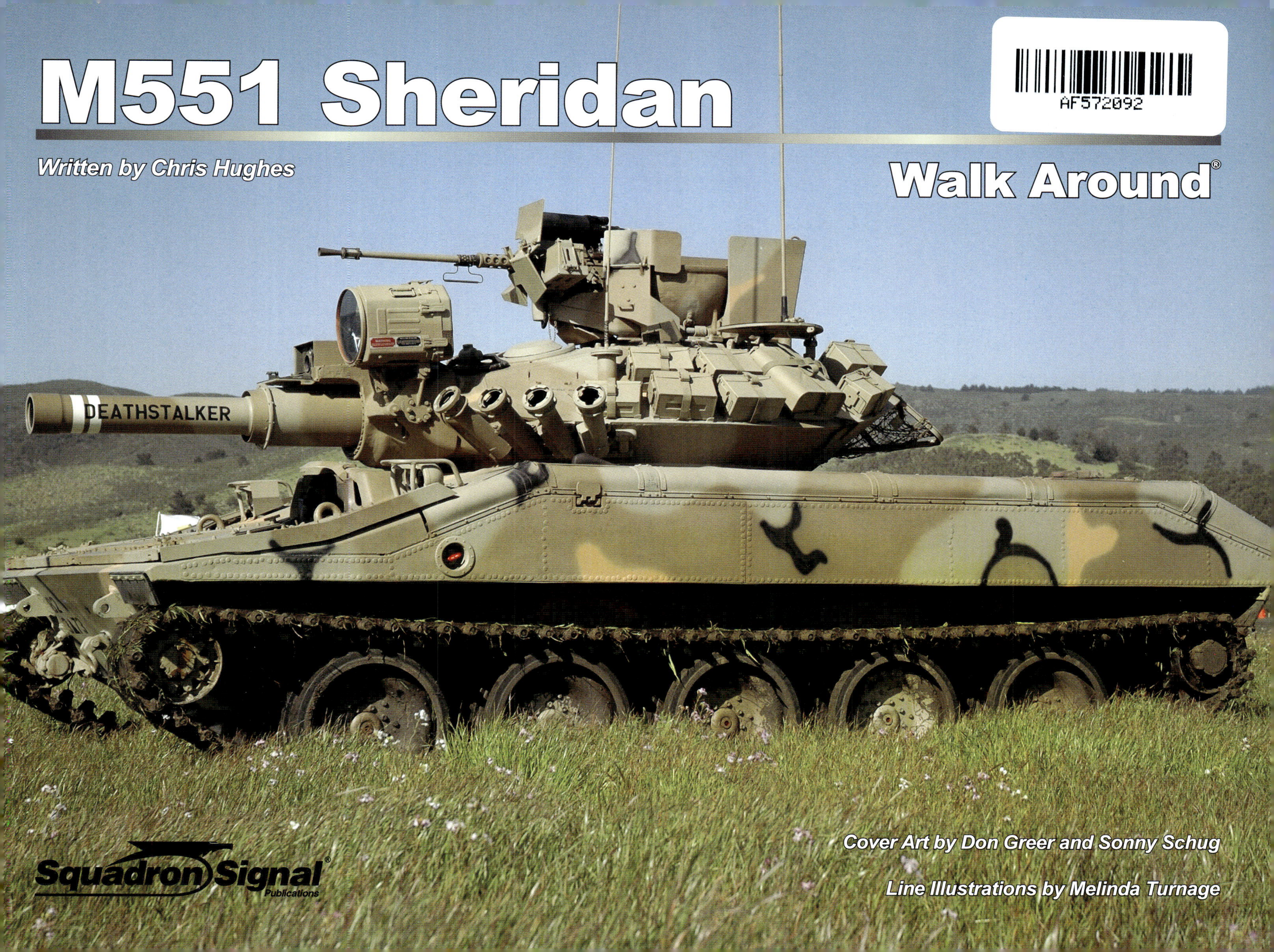

Cover Art by Don Greer and Sonny Schug

Line Illustrations by Melinda Turnage

Squadron/Signal Publications

(Front Cover) An M551 of the 3/4th Cavalry, 25th Infantry Division patrols around Củ Chi, Vietnam, in February 1969. The 3/4th Cavalry was one of the first units in Vietnam to be issued the M551.

(Back Cover) A crewmember of an 82nd Airborne M551A1(TTS) displays his vehicle's basic equipment load during Operation Desert Shield in Saudi Arabia, December 1990.

About the Walk Around® Series

The Walk Around® series is about the details of specific military equipment using color and black-and-white archival and photographs of in-service, preserved, and restored equipment. *Walk Around®* titles are devoted to aircraft and military vehicles. These are picture books focus on operational equipment, not one-off or experimental subjects.

Squadron/Signal Walk Around® books feature the best surviving and restored historic aircraft and vehicles. Inevitably, the requirements of preservation, restoration, exhibit, and continued use may affect these examples in some details of paint and equipment. Authors strive to highlight any feature that departs from original specifications.

Proudly printed in the U.S.A.

1115 Crowley Drive, Carrollton, TX 75006-1312 U.S.A.
www.SquadronSignalPublications.com

Hardcover ISBN 978-0-89747-677-5
Softcover ISBN 978-0-89747-676-8

Military/Combat Photographs and Snapshots

If you have any photos of aircraft, armor, soldiers, or ships of any nation, particularly wartime snapshots, please share them with us and help make Squadron/Signal's books all the more interesting and complete in the future. Any photograph sent to us will be copied and returned. Electronic images are preferred. The donor will be fully credited for any photos used. Please send them to the address above.

(Title Page) The restored M551 belonging to the Military Vehicle Technology Foundation (MVTF) in Portola Valley, California, wears the gray desert MERDEC (Mobility Equipment Research and Development Command) paint scheme of the late 1970s and 1980s.

Acknowledgments

This book is dedicated to the late Jacques M. Littlefield, founder of the Military Vehicle Technology Foundation (MVTF) in Portola Valley, California.

Special thanks are due to the MVTF, home of the M551 *Death Stalker*; to David Doyle for guiding me through this book and other photo projects; to Craig Michelson and Mark Walter at the American Military Museum, a.k.a. "Tankland"; to Brent Sauer, Paul Hannah, and Chuck Sherman for their photos; to Roy Lingle for crucial photos of M551A1 details; and last but not least, to my wife Julie for her patience while I'd go out and get "tanked"!

Introduction

During the early part of 1957, the U.S. Army's Ordnance Committee was in the process of designing a replacement for the 76mm Gun Tank M41. At the time, intelligence reports showed that the Soviet Union was developing its own fully amphibious light tank. The current light tank under development in the United States, the T92, lacked this feature and could not be redesigned to incorporate an amphibious capability. Therefore, new light tank design came about that would be both airborne and amphibious capable.

In 1959, the new light tank was designated the armored reconnaissance/airborne assault vehicle or AR/AAV. In June 1960, Cadillac Motor Car Division received a contract to develop the new AR/AAV. The AR/AAV XM551 was named the Sheridan in August 1961 after Major General Philip H. Sheridan, a Union Army cavalry commander in the American Civil War. The new vehicle was unique in that its main armament consisted of the 152mm XM81 gun-launcher that could fire both the XM13 guided missile or combustible case conventional ammunition.

Twelve pilot vehicles were built by 1965, and in May 1966, the Sheridan was officially standardized for manufacture. Between June 1966 and November 1970, 1,662 M551 Sheridans were produced – all of them at the Cleveland Army Tank Automotive Plant.

Armament of the M551 consisted of the 152mm gun-launcher M81. Secondary armament included either a 7.62mm machine gun M73 or M219 mounted co-axially with the gun-launcher, and a .50-caliber heavy machine gun M2 mounted in the commander's cupola. Weighing just under 16.5 tons combat loaded, the M551 could reach speeds of 43 miles per hour on land. When rigged for amphibious operations, it could attain approximately 3.5 miles per hour in calm water

The M551 was first deployed in combat in Vietnam in February 1969. The vehicle also served with U.S. armored cavalry regiments stationed in West Germany during the Cold War. Beginning in 1972, a laser range finder system was procured for the Sheridan. Vehicles so fitted were designated AR/AAV M551A1. In 1977, a further series of modifications came in the form of a Product Improvement Program or PIP that included various power pack improvements, a stronger drive sprocket mount, and new steel tow lugs to replace the aluminum ones that had a tendency to shear off under high stress loads. In spite of the modifications, the M551 was still plagued by problems with the M81 gun-launcher system and various maintenance issues. These led to the vehicle being withdrawn from all active Army units, other than the 82nd Airborne Division, since the M551 was the only armored vehicle in the Army's inventory that could be air dropped.

With the 82nd Airborne, the M551 saw combat during the U.S. invasion of Panama in December 1989 and in Saudi Arabia and Kuwait during the war against Iraq, code named Operation Desert Shield/Desert Storm in 1990 and 1991. It also formed the basis of a series of visual modification (VISMOD) vehicles that were built to look like Soviet-bloc equipment. After the M551 was retired from service with the 82nd Airborne in 1996, the VISMODs remained in service at the National Training Center (NTC) at Ft. Irwin, California, and the Joint Readiness Training Center (JRTC) at Ft. Polk, Louisiana, until 2003, at which time all M551 types were withdrawn from service.

Built by the Allison Division of Cadillac Motors starting in 1966, the M551 was in service with the U.S. Army for over 35 years, with the last of the vehicles being retired in 2003.

Many M551s finished their careers with visual modification (VISMOD) kits for use at the National Training Center (NTC) at Ft. Irwin, California, or the Joint Readiness Training Center (JRTC) at Ft. Polk, Louisiana. This Sheridan was modified to simulate a Soviet T-72 main battle tank. (Charles Sherman)

A compensating idler wheel is positioned at the front of the tank on each side. Each wheel consists of an inner and outer idler wheel with an idler hub sandwiched in between them. They are held together with 22 self-locking bolts.

Lacking rubber tires, the idler wheels are a natural metal color wherever they meet the track shoes. The inner rims of each wheel are burnished to a sheen after recent contact with the track shoe's guide teeth.

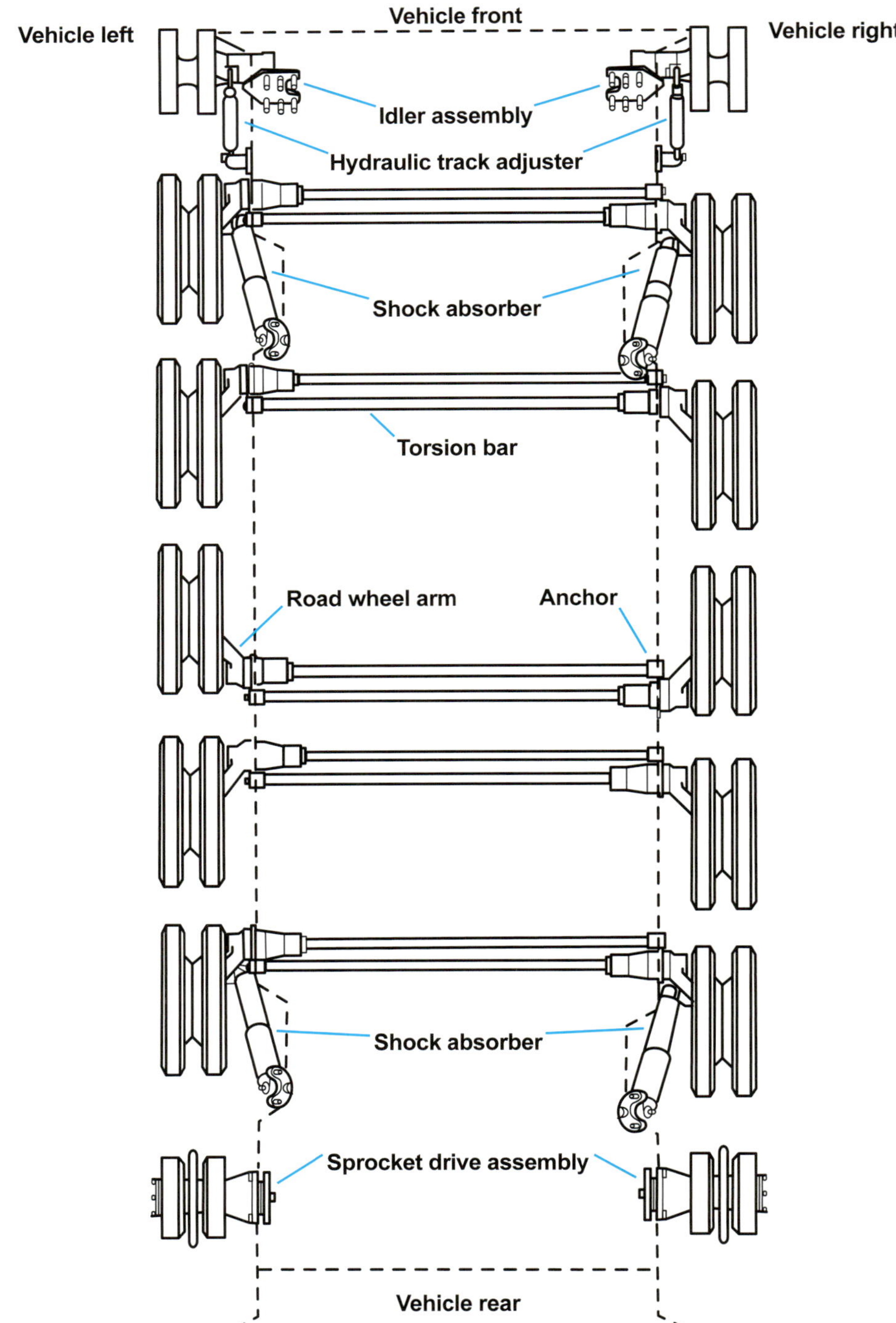

Idler Shaft and Housing Group

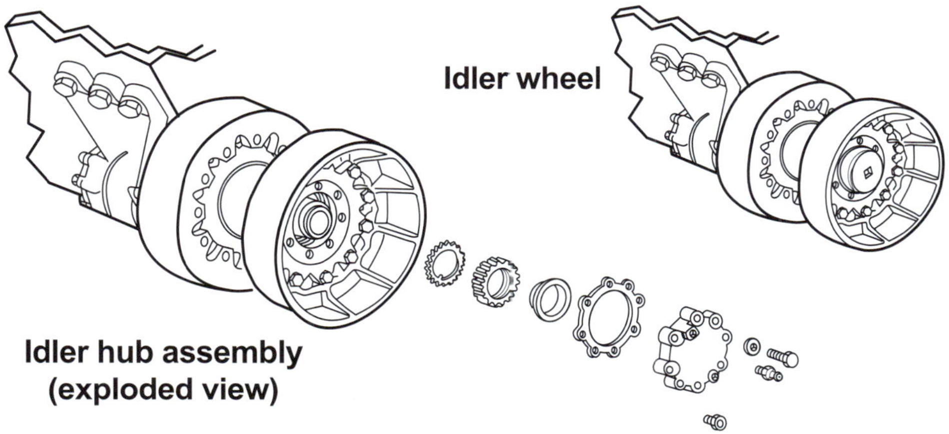

Idler wheel

Idler hub assembly (exploded view)

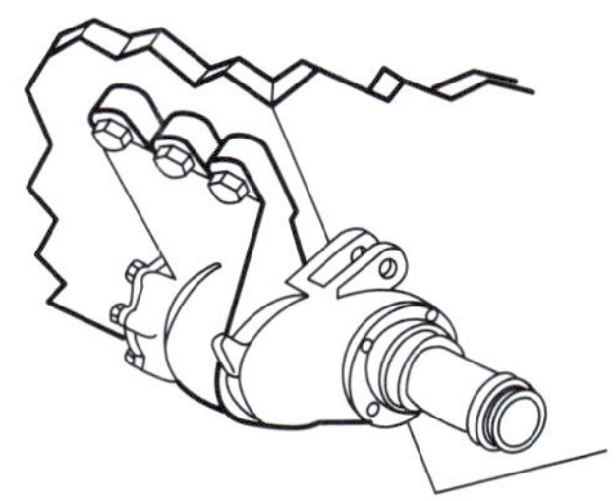

Idler shaft and housing

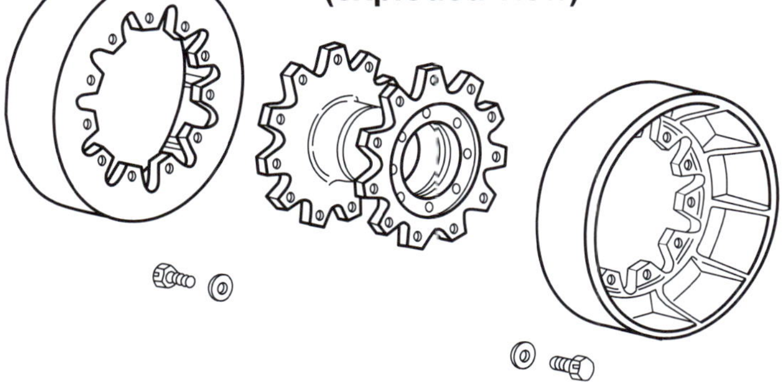

Idler wheel (exploded view)

Grease has seeped out of the lubrication fitting (in red) on the right side idler housing and stained the area around it. The housings are attached to the hull with four screws and two bolts. The linkage for the right side track adjuster can be seen to the left of the lubrication fitting.

A circular access cover keeps the sleeve bearings and idler shaft in the idler housing. Eight screws hold the cover in place.

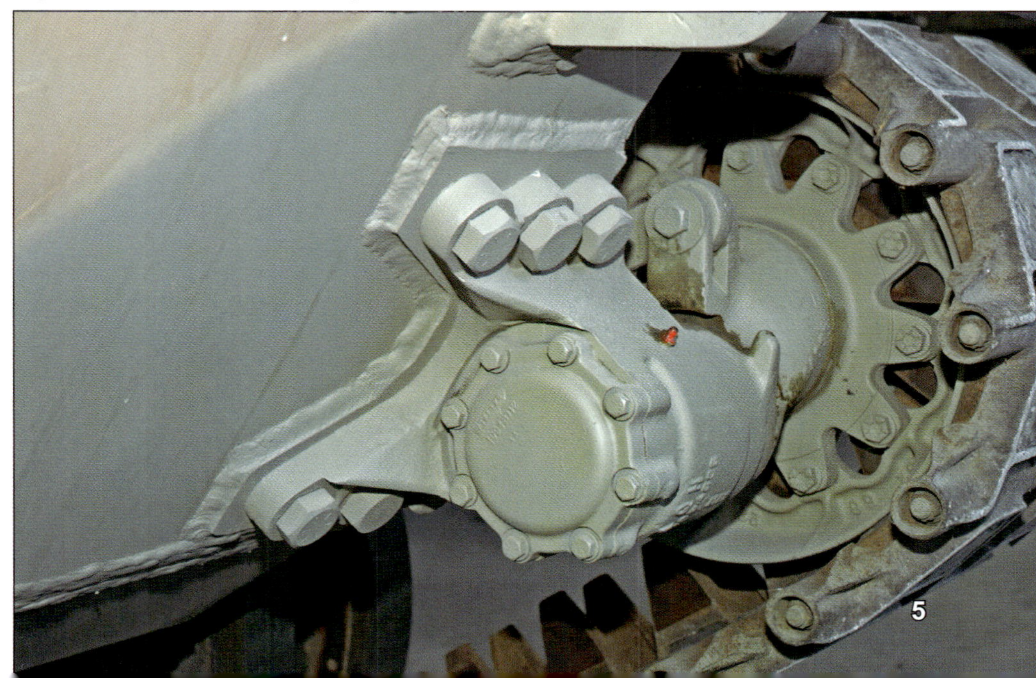

The M551 runs on T138 single-pin tracks. Each track shoe has two rubber pads on the ground contact side. The shoes on this MVTF M551 show signs of recent wear.

While most of the metal portions of this track are rusted, the outer edges of the guide teeth have been worn down to bare metal from recent contact with the inner edges of the road wheels and idler wheels.

The rubber pads on the T138 tracks are not replaceable. Once they have been worn out, the entire track shoe must be replaced. The circle on the inside of each track guide tooth is the logo of the factory that cast the tracks.

Extreme wear of the track pads results in actual pieces of the pad separating from the metal track shoe.

The M551 rides on 20 rubber tired road wheels – five two-wheeled sets on each side of the tank. Twenty-four reinforcement rivets line the outer rim of each wheel, while eight self-locking bolts secure the wheels to the hub. Eight screws mate the two wheels in each set to each other. There is a red-painted grease fitting in the center of the wheel. The outer faces of the track guide teeth are shiny due to contact with the inner sides of the road wheels.

Mud and debris can build up in the space between the two road wheels. A wear flange encircles the inner rim of each wheel. The track shoe guide teeth rub on the wear flange instead of the actual wheels, thereby prolonging the life of the wheels.

A hydraulic track adjuster is fitted to each idler assembly. Adding grease to the adjuster via the red painted grease fitting tightens track tension. Opening the pressure bleed plug below it reduces tension in the track. Below the hydraulic track adjuster is one of 14 air-drop tiedown brackets.

Each road wheel is mounted on a suspension-arm assembly. Grease-stained dirt covers the road wheel arm access cover while a red painted lubrication fitting shows through near the top of the arm.

Mud build up such as this could lead to a thrown track if not properly cleaned. Maintenance in the field by the crew was always important to keep the vehicle operational.

Shock Absorber Assembly

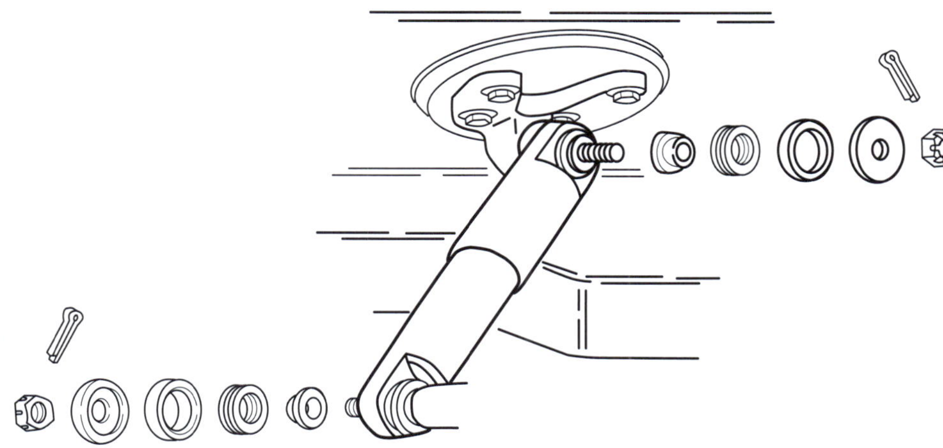

Shock absorbers are fitted to the front and rear road wheel arms on each side of the M551. The lower portion of the shock absorber is attached to the bottom of the road wheel arm and secured in place by a slotted nut and cotter pin.

The upper portion of the shock absorber is attached to a mounting bracket on the side of the hull. Four screws secure the mounting bracket to a circular disk that is welded to the hull.

Stacked in order on the bolt, behind the slotted nut and cotter pin, are a shock absorber cover, a seal, a resilient mount, and a spacer.

This exploded view shows the composition of the drive sprocket assembly with two carrier wheels on the outside, the sprocket and the sprocket hub in the center. A total of 22 self-locking bolts, 11 on each side, secure the hub to the wheels. Eleven nuts and bolts secure the hub to the sprocket.

Sprocket Drive Assembly

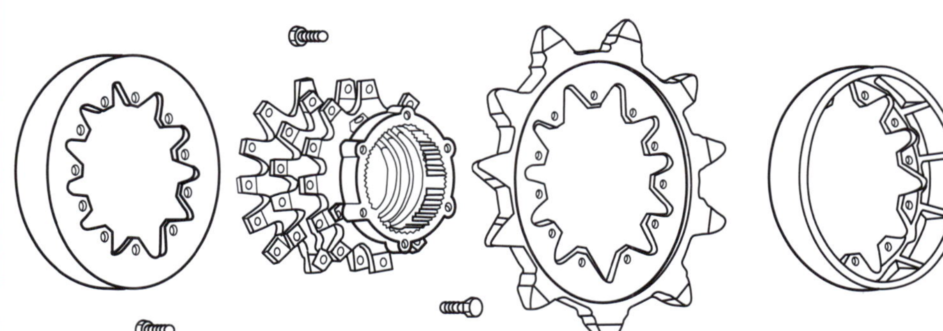

Each road wheel arm is mounted on a torsion bar. The opposite end of each torsion bar is covered on the other side of the hull by a torsion bar anchor. The torsion bar anchor is held in place by two bolts and a length of lockwire.

Fourteen air-drop tiedown brackets are screwed on to the M551, seven on each side of the hull. They are located between each road wheel station, and behind the drive sprocket. The tiedowns are used to strap the M551 to the air-drop platform.

The drive sprockets are mounted at the back of the hull. Each sprocket assembly consists of a drive sprocket and sprocket hub sandwiched between two sprocket carrier wheels. Six screws hold the access cover to the front of the outer sprocket carrier wheel.

There is wear on the on the parts of the sprocket carrier hubs that contact the track shoe pads. When the sprocket teeth have worn down by ⅜ of an inch, the drive sprocket needs to be replaced.

Combat loaded, the M551 weighs 33,460 pounds. Designed with air transportability in mind, the small size of the M551 made it suitable to be carried by the C130 Hercules. The M551 series of tanks, which was used exclusively by the U.S. Army, saw combat in Vietnam, Panama (Operation Just Cause), and Iraq (Operation Desert Storm).

When an AN/VVG-1 laser range finder has been added to a Sheridan commander's cupola, the vehicle is designated as an M551A1. The transceiver is the rectangular box located beneath the .50-caliber machine gun mount. It replaced the front vision block of the cupola. (Paul Hannah)

Between the end of June 1966, when the first two production vehicles were built, and November 1970, when the last M551 was accepted, 1,662 Sheridans were produced.

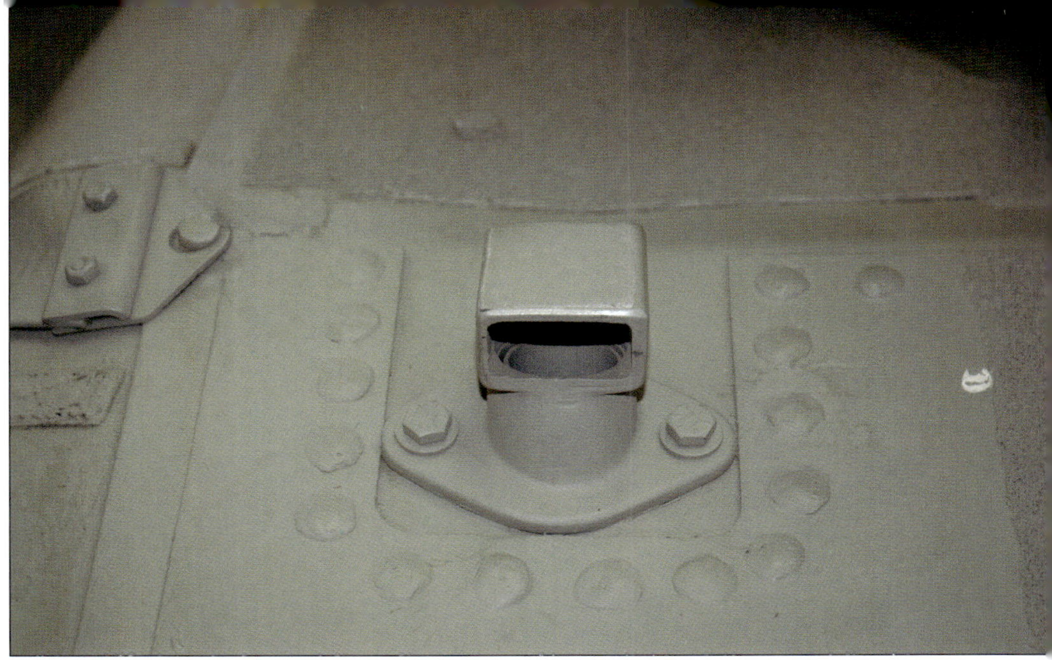

A small personnel heater is located in the right side of the driver's compartment. Its exhaust outlet is on the right side of the glacis, behind the right headlight assembly.

In front of the personnel heater exhaust outlet is the right headlight assembly. The headlight has both white and infrared light lenses. A blackout drive light is located under a hood between the two main lenses. A blackout marker light is contained in the slot below the main lenses.

A tubular brush guard for the headlight assembly is bolted to the glacis and protects the headlight assembly from damage caused by debris when out in the field. It also serves to lessen the chance of a vehicle crewmember stepping on the headlight assembly and damaging it.

A lifting eye is bolted to the glacis in front of the right headlight assembly. An identical eye is mounted in front of the left headlight assembly. These eyes are used in conjunction with two rear lifting eyes when hoisting the vehicle for transport.

When the driver openes the hatch, it rotates behind his head and is stored in a housing that has been cast into the glacis plate.

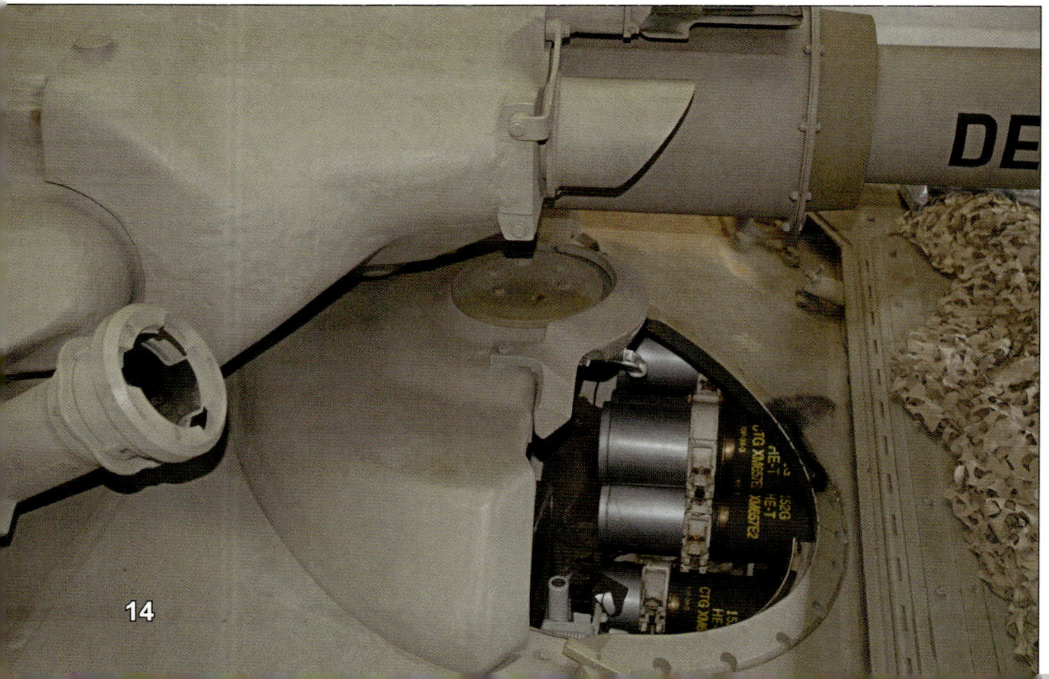

The driver's seat is in the center of the glacis underneath a rotating hatch cover. When closing the hatch cover, the driver rotates it clockwise, as viewed from his position.

Three M47 periscopes are mounted in the driver's rotating hatch cover for use when it is closed. For nighttime operations, the center M47 periscope would be replaced with an infrared compatible M48 periscope. (Mark Walter)

Resting on the glacis is the vehicle's surfboard. This collapsible, two-piece board was used in conjunction with the flotation barrier when it was erected. Since the surfboard would block the driver's vision when it was raised, a window is provided in each section for him to use when driving on land or in the water.

The freeboard of the M551 with the surfboard and floatation barrier erected was 24 inches at the top of the barrier when the vehicle was floating.

Two windows for the driver were provided the front of the surfboard. The driver used the lower window when entering or exiting the water, while he used the upper window while the vehicle was actually in the water.

Two retainers hold down the surfboard when it is folded flat on the glacis. A non-slip surface texture is applied to exterior portions of the surfboard and other parts of the upper hull.

This M551 with the swim barrier erected shows the placement of the driver's windows in the surfboard. (Patton Museum via David Doyle)

The two aluminum towing lugs welded to the bow of the M551 are used in conjunction with either tow cables or tow bars. When used with cables, a clevis would be inserted through the cable loop and bolted to the lug.

Overstressing of the aluminum tow lugs often resulted in one or both being sheared off of the hull like the one seen in this example. (Mark Walter)

Multiple weld beads are used to attach the towing lug to the bow. However, field reports indicated that the welds were too weak to support the M551 when being towed.

Beginning in 1977, a Product Improvement Program (PIP) was started to correct certain problems found on the M551. One improvement included replacing the original aluminum tow lugs with steel ones bolted to the hull using a steel backing plate. (Mark Walter)

The driver's escape hatch cover is slightly in front of the driver's seat and can only be opened from inside the vehicle.

The outside lens of each headlight assembly projects an infrared beam and is used with the driver's M48 infrared night vision periscope.

The headlight assembly plugs into a mount assembly. It is secured to the mount with a clamp. Four screws attach the headlight guard to the hull.

Five screws at the headlight mount base adjust the headlight horizontally. Vertical adjustment is accomplished by turning three screws on the lower rear of the headlight.

A staff member puts the Sheridan from the Military Vehicle Technology Foundation through its paces in a grassy field. The M551 could travel on level road at speeds up to 43 miles per hour and had a road range of approximately 350 miles.

Rubber fenders are bolted to the front of the tank over each track run. They help reduce the amount of dust and water spray kicked up by the tank as it moves.

The extreme slope of the glacis can be seen in this view of the left, front of the hull. Angling the armor helps deflect incoming fire from penetrating the tank. The fire extinguisher pull handle is located in the side of the hull.

A fire extinguisher pull handle is located on the left front side of the hull. It operates the fire extinguishers mounted inside the crew compartments.

The hull of the M551 is made from welded plates of 7039 aluminum alloy armor. To increase the buoyancy of the M551, a layer of high-density foam surrounds the hull. A thin layer of aluminum covers the foam itself.

A fabric flotation barrier is stored along the upper edges of the upper hull. A series of barrier covers keep it stored until needed. Retaining straps bolted to the lower edge of the covers secure them closed.

Flotation Barrier Stowage Covers

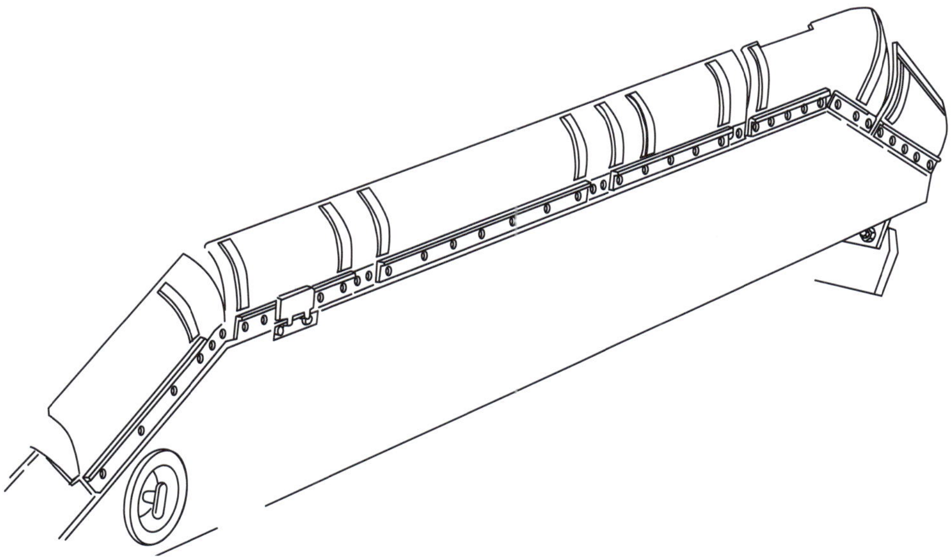

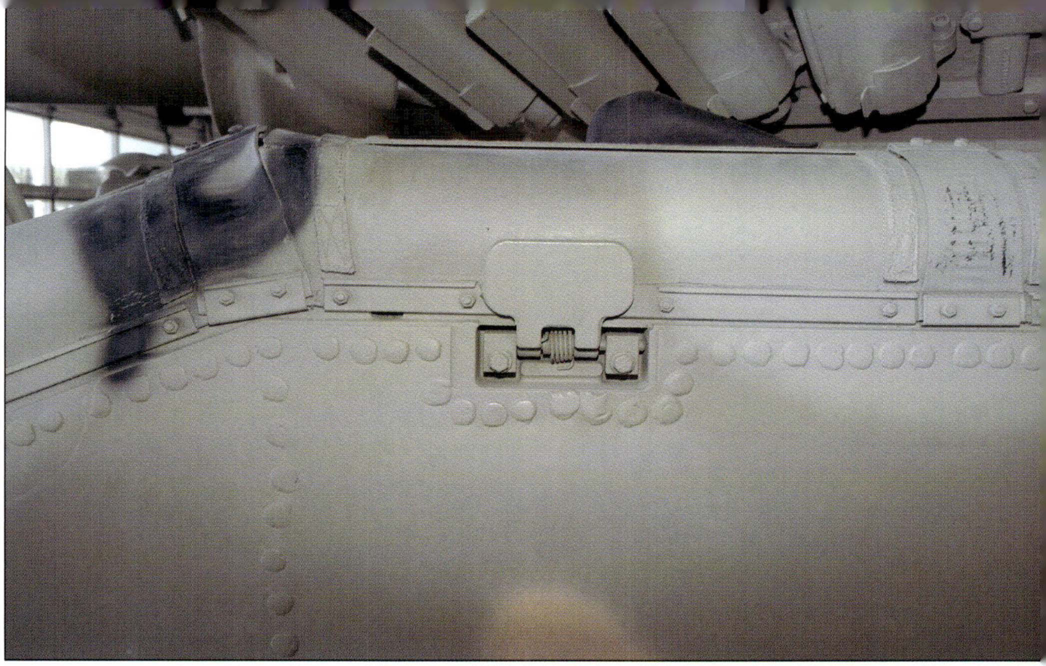

Mounted on each side of the hull near the front of the Sheridan is a crew step that helps crewmembers climb over the erected floatation barrier.

The front bilge pump elbow is mounted on the left side of the hull, above the crew step. When the flotation barrier is erected, the elbow is removed and a tube is inserted in its place. The tube extends upwards above the barrier and water from the bilge pump is ejected from the tank through it.

Pioneer tools are stored on the upper, rear hull of the M551. Bilge outlets are located below each of the upper hull lifting eyes. Additional towing lugs and a towing pintle are attached to the lower hull rear. Five large and two canvas straps are used to secure the collapsed barrier screen to the upper hull rear.

The left taillight assembly is mounted in the intercommunication set access door. Above and to the left of the taillight is the call indicator light.

When illuminated, the call indicator light lets accompanying infantry know that someone in the tank would like to talk to them via the C-2296/VRC external control box.

The door is latched closed with a spring-loaded handle. Lifting the handle releases the latch and allows the door to be opened.

A C-2296/VRC external control box and hand set allow the crew to communicate with accompanying infantry without exposing themselves to enemy fire.

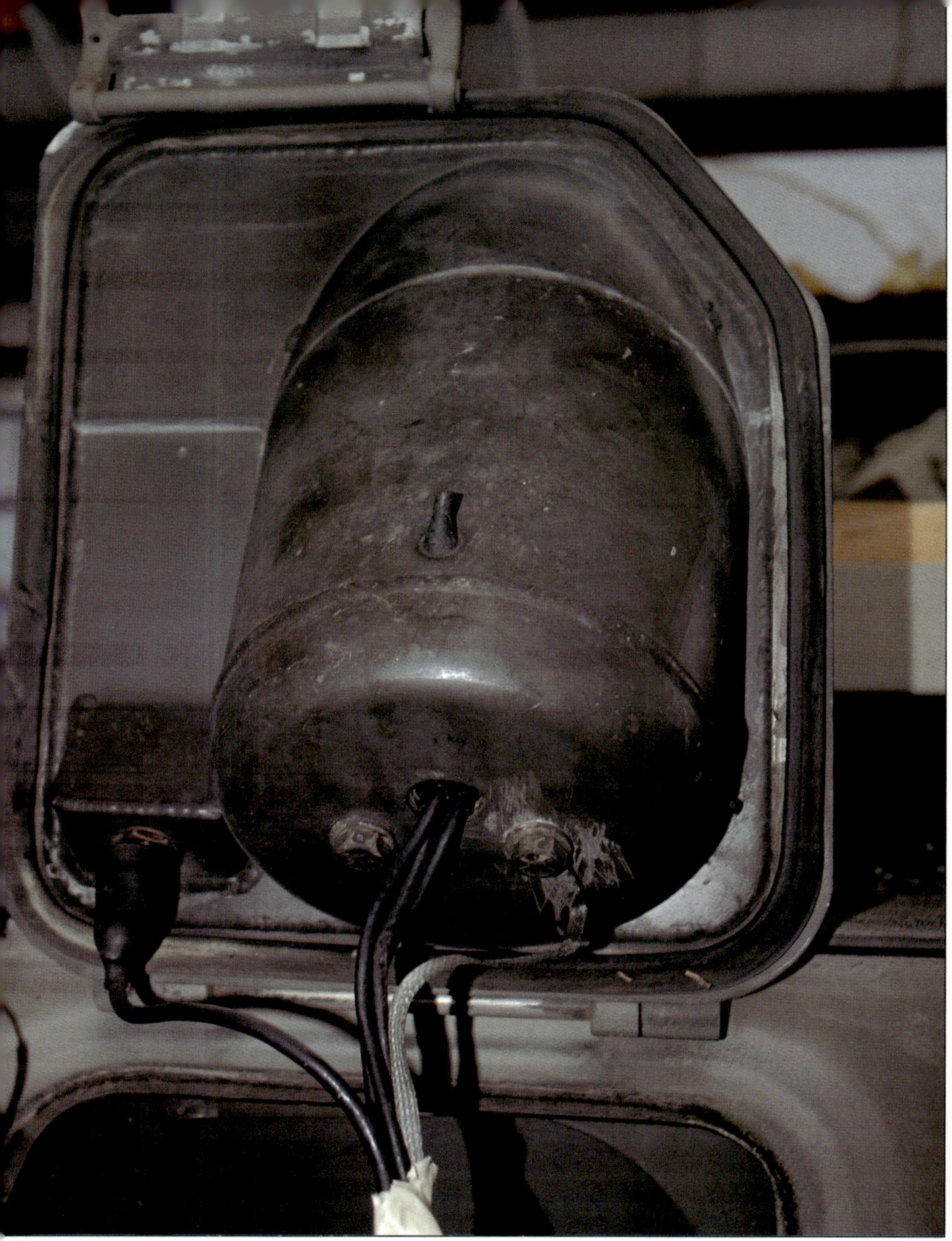

A bulged housing is formed into the access door. Wiring for both the taillight assembly and call light hang downwards from the housing. These wires connect to components inside the compartment.

A lifting eye is attached to the hull above and to the right of the left hand side bilge outlet housing. Another lifting eye is bolted above and to the left of the right hand side bilge outlet housing.

A hull bilge outlet housing is located below the left, rear lifting eye. The rear bilge pumps remove water from the engine compartment during amphibious operations. Like the forward bilge outlet, a tube assembly was inserted in the outlet when the barrier was raised and water was removed from the engine compartment through the tube.

Rear Bilge Pump Outlet Hose Assembly

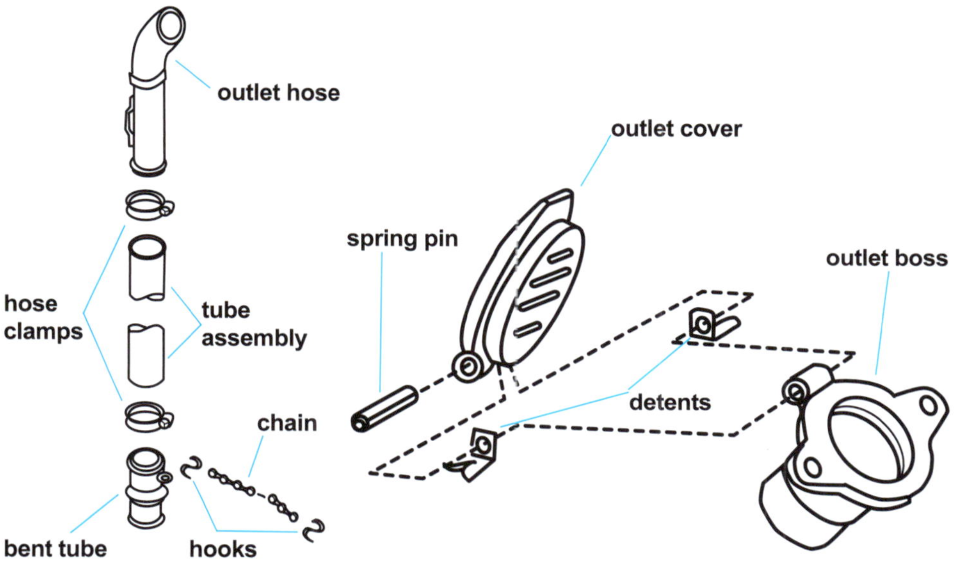

An identical bilge pump outlet is located on the right, rear of the hull below the right, rear-lifting eye. Above it and to the right is the right side taillight assembly.

When the engine compartment bilge pump is used, the outlet cover is opened in order to insert the outlet hose assembly. To the left of the bilge outlet is the right, rear lifting eye.

The right side taillight consists of a blackout marker light on top and a service taillight on the bottom.

The engine exhaust outlet sits on the rear edge of the engine deck and vents exhaust gases out towards the back of the vehicle.

Even running the vehicle for only a short period of time leaves a sooty exhaust residue on the pioneer tools that are mounted on the rear of the M551. The pioneer tools are themselves mounted on the rear engine access plate.

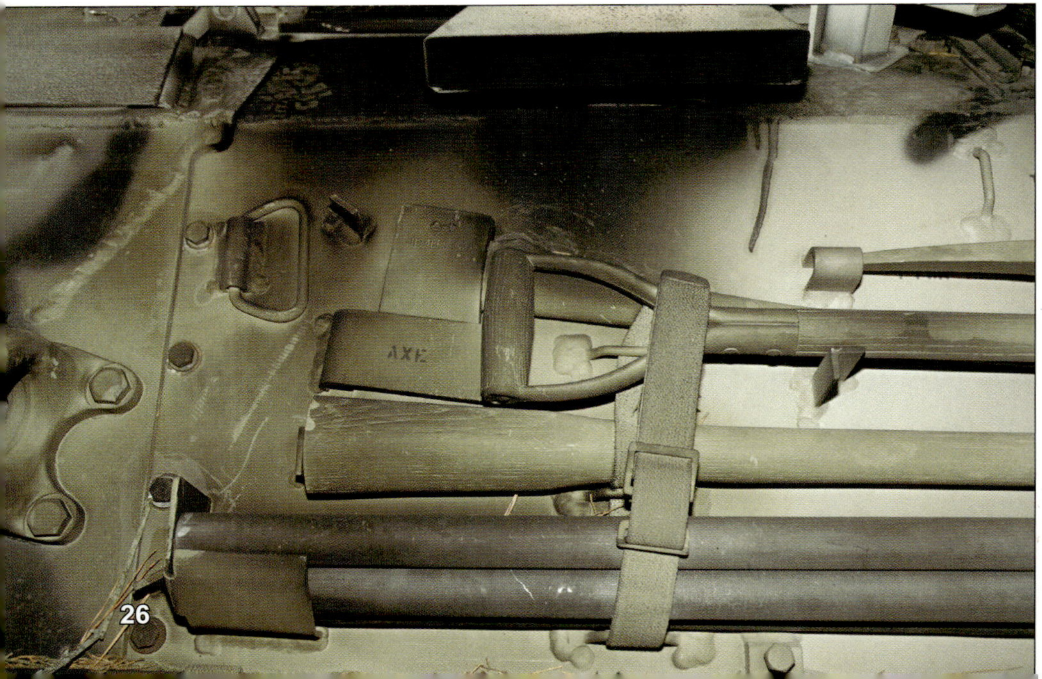

The shovel and main armament cleaning staffs are among the tools stored on the rear engine access plate. Footman loops for the storage straps used to secure the tools are welded to various points on the access door.

Below the pioneer tools is the rear floatation barrier cover. Straps are buckled over the cover to keep it closed when the barrier is not in use.

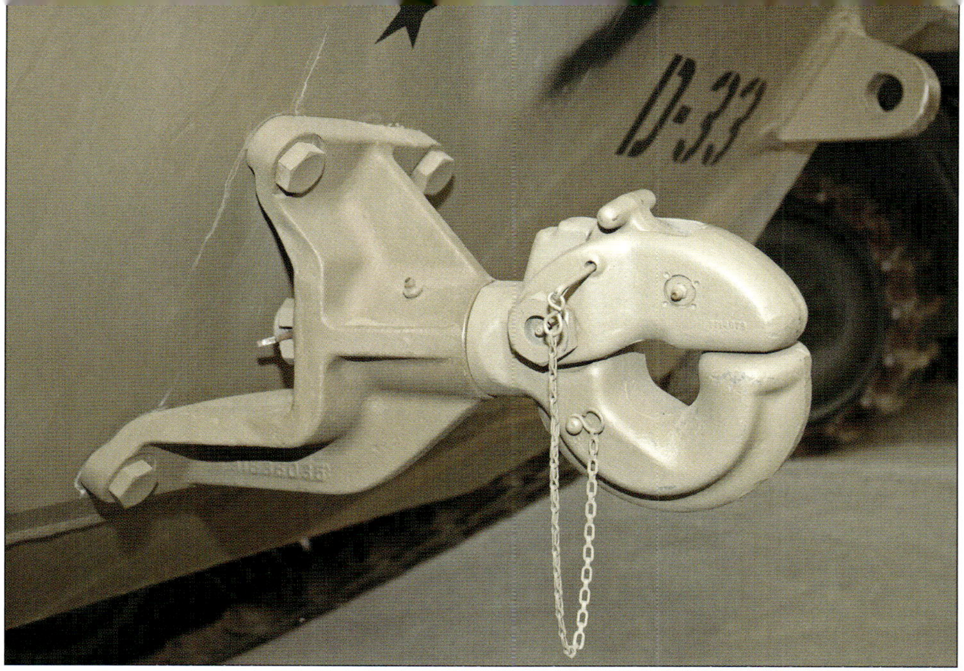

The towing pintle bracket is mounted on the lower rear of the hull with four screws. The actual towing pintle assembly is attached to the bracket with a slotted screw and cotter pin. When using a tow bar, the tow bar ring is hooked onto the pintle.

This view of the right, rear air-drop tiedown bracket reveals the multiple weld beads used to assemble the hull rear plate to the side of the hull.

Rubber fenders or mud flaps are bolted to a metal strip that is welded to the bottom of the hull overhang on the rear of the track run. They help cut down the amount of dust and mud kicked up by the tracks when the vehicle is in motion.

Another prominent weld shows were the lower, rear hull plate joins the belly plate. The transmission drain plug is located just below the weld.

A bustle rack for storing crew equipment is mounted on the rear of the turret. Three engine grilles and debris screens are located on the engine deck. The grille underneath the turret bustle is the engine compartment air intake grillem, while the two grilles in the foreground are the engine compartment exhaust grilles.

Hot air from the engine and transmission is vented out of the two grilles on the rear of the engine deck. A locking pin located between the two grilles keeps them closed. A lifting handle for each grille is located next to the locking pin.

Cooling air is drawn into the engine compartment through a large grille at the front of the engine deck. The grille assembly weighs over 70 pounds and would normally be removed with a lifting sling attached to the four lifting handles, two of which are seen on the left.

Each exhaust grille assembly consists of a grille covered by a debris screen, multiple screws, cotter pins, washers, and a locking pin. The engine exhaust outlet is located to the left of the grille in this photo.

The two exhaust grilles both open outwards from the engine deck. Opening up the grilles allows the crew to access the engine for Preventive Maintenance Checks and Services (PMCS). Debris screens are fixed to the grilles to prevent foreign objects from entering the compartment and damaging the engine.

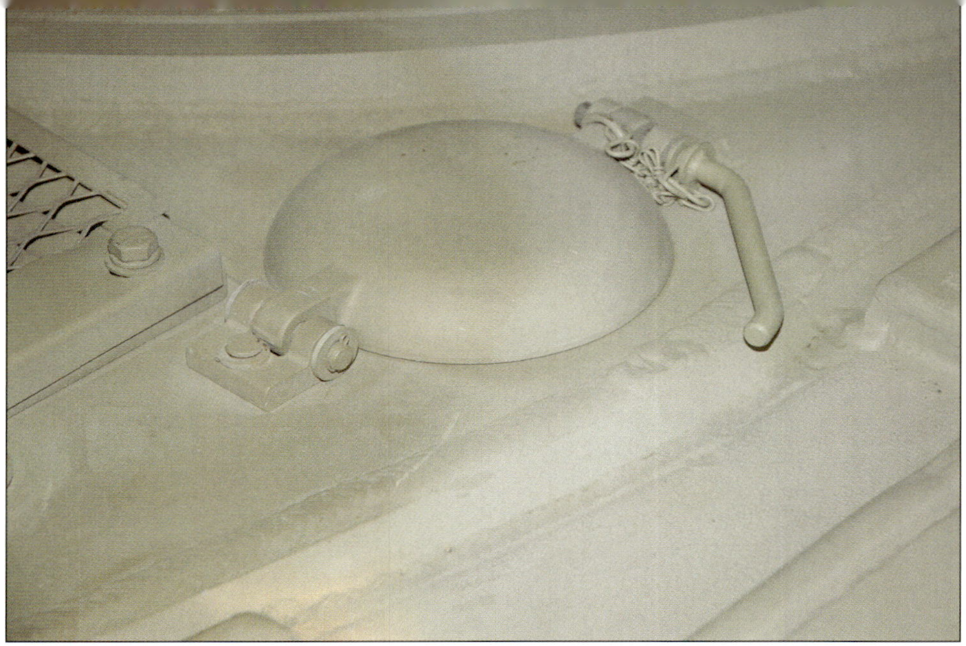

The battery access door is located on the right side of the engine deck. Keeping it closed are two door pin assemblies located on the outer edges of the door. The door opens up and towards the front of the vehicle. A non-slip coating covers most of the flat surfaces of the deck.

Each fuel filler cover is hinged at the rear and locked closed with an angled pin assembly. The covers open towards the rear of the tank. A small chain is attached to the pin and filler cover to prevent it from being lost.

The M551 is equipped with two fuel tanks, which hold a total of 158 gallons of Diesel fuel. A fuel filler cap and cover are located on each side of the tank near the air intake grille like the left side one seen here.

A wire-lifting handle is fitted to the top of the filler cap for the crew to use when removing the cap. Like the fuel filler cover pin, a chain is attached to the inside of the filler cap to prevent it from being lost when the cap is unscrewed. A screen is located inside the fuel filler to filter out any solid material that may be in the fuel.

The two-piece access door for the engine air cleaner is located underneath the left side of the engine deck.

The door opens upwards to allow the crew to access the air cleaner for maintenance. This vehicle had an exhaust manifold leak, which built up soot in this area.

The battery compartment access doors are located under the right side of the engine deck. Vehicle tools are stored here as well.

The battery access door is hinged at the bottom and opens downwards. A pair of commercial 12-volt batteries are used in this vehicle.

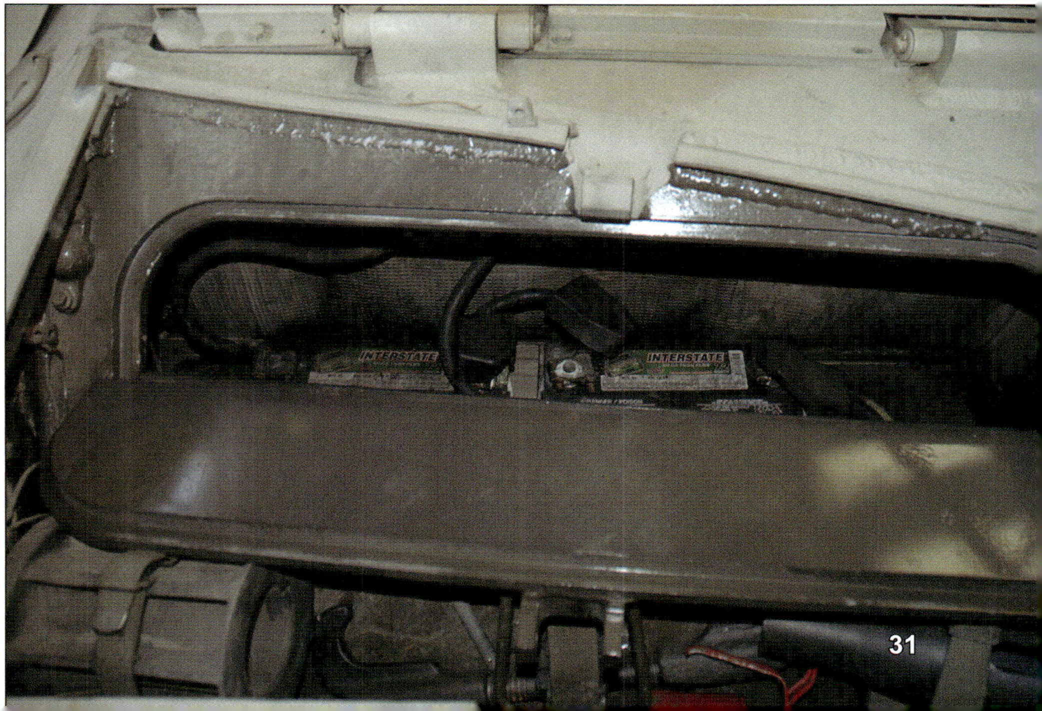

A General Motors 6V53T six-cylinder, two-cycle, turbosupercharged Diesel engine powers the M551. The white cylinder is the coolant surge tank. The black and red housing behind the surge tank is the supercharger, while the transmission oil level gage is between the two.

Coupled to the 6V53T is the Allison XTG-250-1A transmission. The XTG-250-1A is a six-speed transmission with four speeds forward and two reverse.

In the front of the engine compartment is the radiator cooling fan. The spring in the foreground is the belt tensioner.

The transmission shift control is located on top of the transmission. A shift control cable is attached at one end to the shift quadrant in the driver's compartment and runs through the right side of the hull until it terminates here. The orange object on the upper right is the turbocharger.

On display at the 82nd Airborne Division War Memorial Museum, Ft Bragg, North Carolina, this M551A1 wears the NATO three-tone camouflage in which 82nd Airborne Division M551A1s finished their service careers. (Paul Hannah)

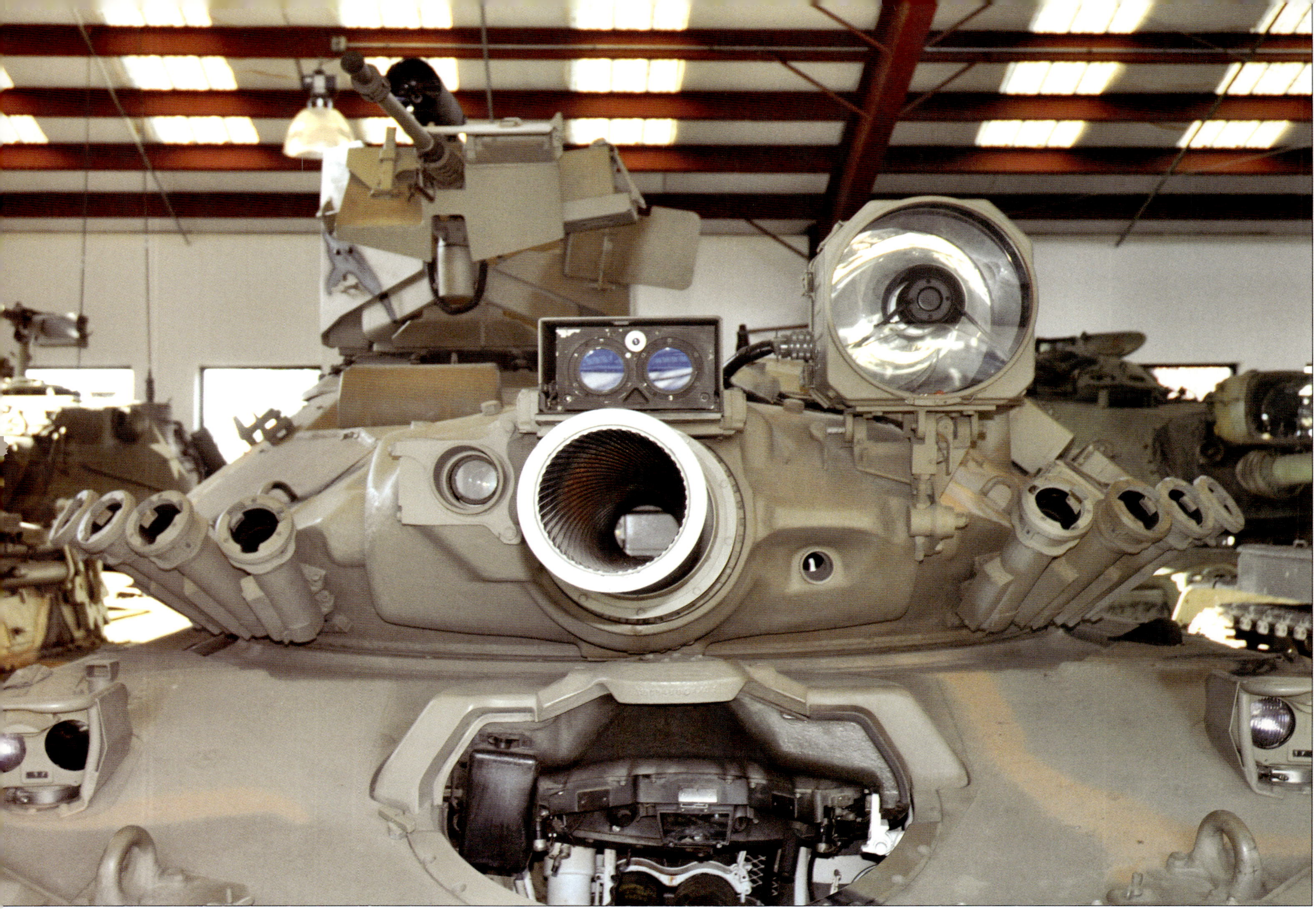

The main armament of the M551 is the 152mm Gun Launcher M81E1. Using the MGM51A Shillelagh missile, it could engage targets at a distance of 2,000 meters or 3,000 meters with the extended-range MGM51B. With HEAT and HE-T rounds the maximum range was 9,000 meters.

The gunner's telescopic sight aperture is located on the right side of the gun shield. A sun/rain shield helps prevent the sight lense from being obscured. Above the main gun tube is the optical transmitter box for the missile.

Three bolts attach the sight shield to the gun shield. A rubber plug can be inserted into the aperture when the sight is not in use.

This side view of the gun shield reveals the curved contours of the gun shield casting. The tubular sun/rain shield for the gunner's sight is seen in the center of the photo.

The port for the co-axial 7.62mm machine gun is located on the lower, left side of the gun shield. The 7.62mm M73 machine gun was used in early production vehicles. It was later superceded by the M73E1 and finally, the 7.62mm M219 machine gun.

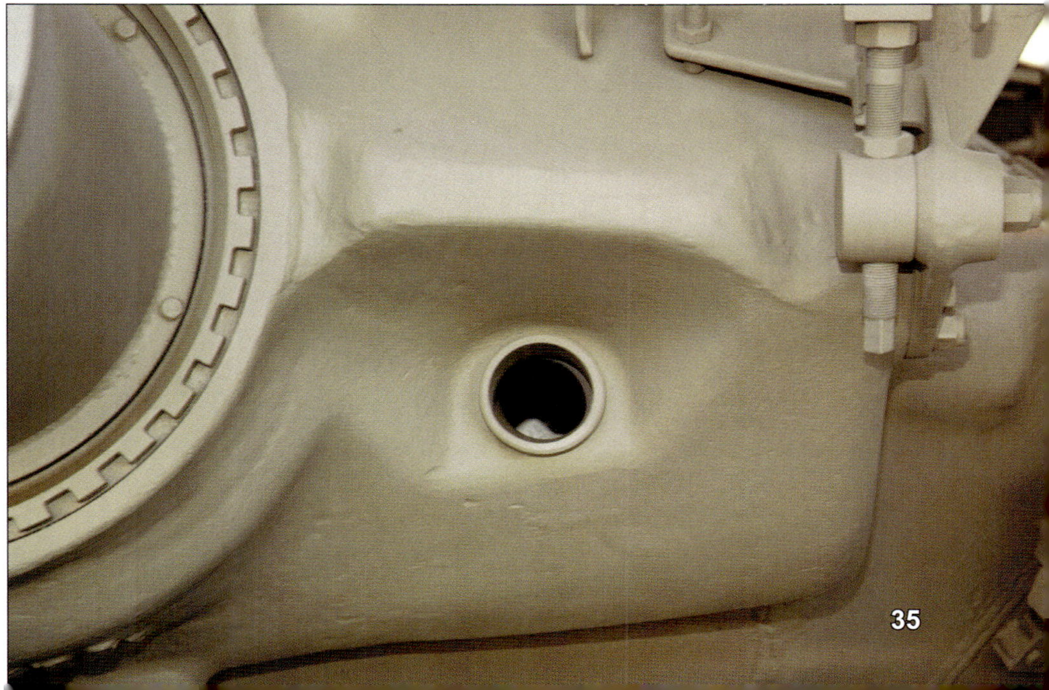

The optical transmitter box is mounted on the gun shield above the main gun. Infrared guidance signals from the box guide the Shillelagh missile towards its target.

For night fighting, the M551 is equipped with an AN/VSS-3 searchlight. Mounted on the left side of the gun shield, it can project both white and infrared light beams.

With its cover open, the infrared transmitter lenses of the optical transmitter box are revealed.

Power for the light is supplied via a cable that plugs into the right side of the light unit. There is a lifting handle located on the upper portion of the light unit.

The power cable for the searchlight connects to an outlet on top of the turret. When not in use, the outlet is protected from the elements by a screw-on cover.

Three mounting pins secure the searchlight mount to the vehicle support. Weighing 73 pounds, the searchlight is a two-man lift when it comes to hoisting it onto or off of its mounting bracket.

Latches on the rear and sides of the searchlight case allow the rear cover to be removed for maintenance of the light. Cooling vents are built into the rear cover of the light case.

The 152mm M81E1 fires both the MGM-51A/B Shillelagh missile and various types of combustible case conventional ammunition. The length of the gun tube and chamber is 105.1 inches or 17.5 calibers.

A total of eight XM176 grenade launchers are mounted on the front of the turret: four on the left and four on the right. The launchers can be fired singly, in groups of four, or all eight at one time.

The rifled barrel has 48 grooves with a uniform right hand twist. A keyway is located at the six o'clock position of the bore. The key on the Shillelagh missile fit into this keyway to prevent the missile from spinning as it traveled down the barrel.

The turret consists of rolled homogeneous steel armor plates, welded together. Brackets for the .50-caliber M2 machine gun cradle are welded to the left side of the turret. A lifting eye is seen near the forward weld bead.

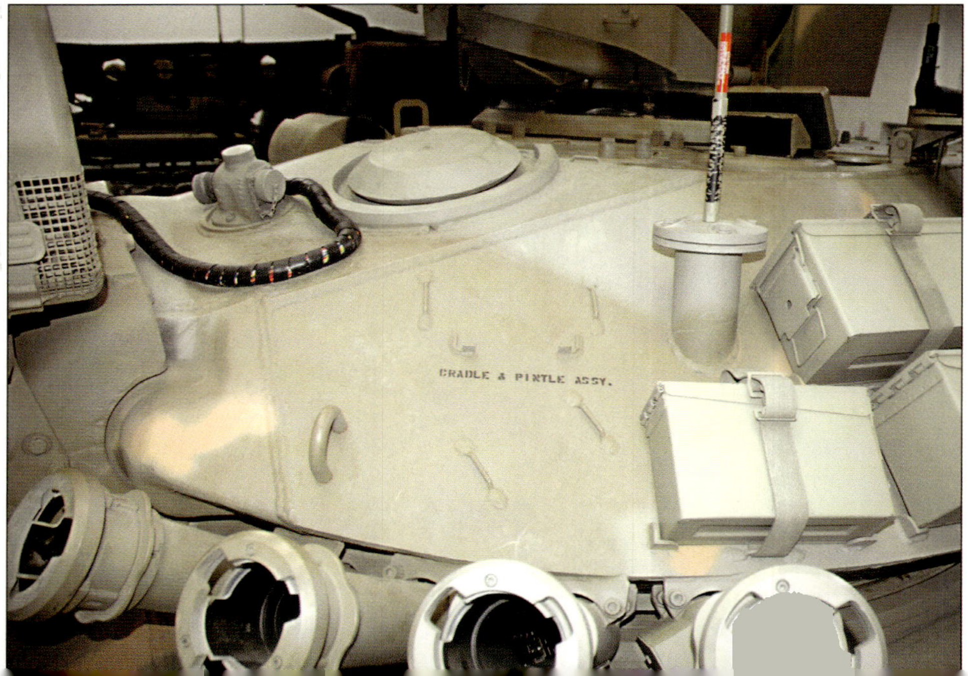

The small size of the Sheridan leaves little interior storage space. Six ammunition boxes for the commander's .50-caliber M2 machine gun and the co-axial 7.62mm machine gun are strapped to the left side of the turret. In addition to the ammunition cans, a water can is also strapped to the turret side.

When not mounted on the commander's cupola, the machine gun pintle support is fitted into a bracket next to the water can on the left side of the turret. This is especially true when the vehicle is rigged for an air drop.

Additional equipment is stored in the bustle racks at the rear of the turret. A mesh net helps keep the equipment in place.

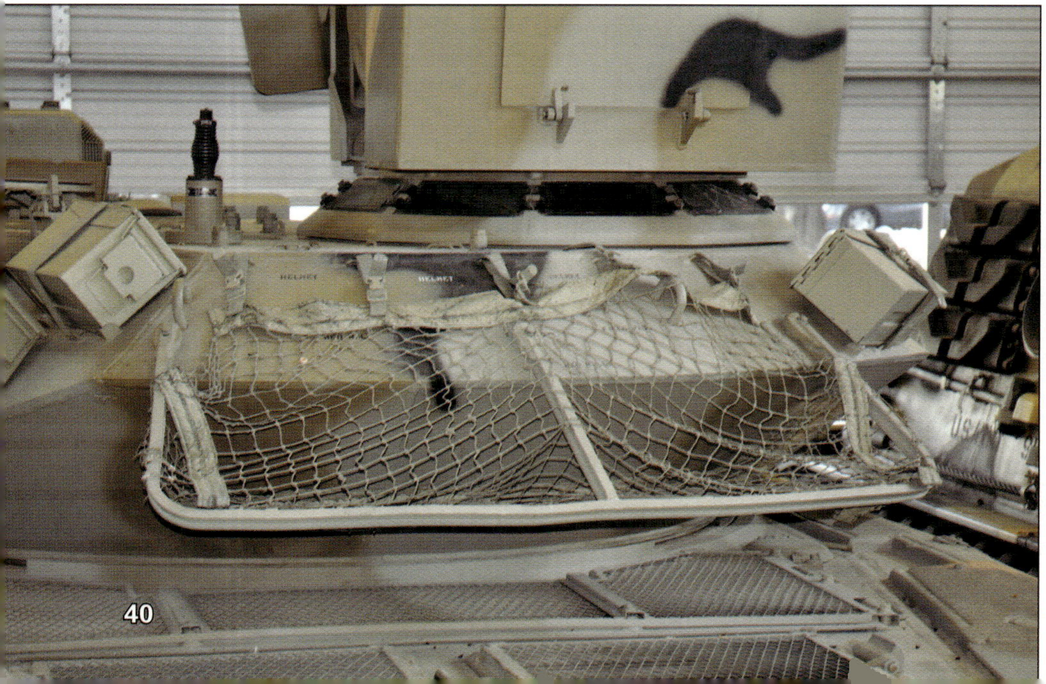

During the mid-1980's, M551A1 vehicles in the 82nd Airborne Division were fitted with a larger bustle rack. (Brent Sauer)

With the bustle rack removed, the rear turret lifting eyes can be seen. Four footman loops for hanging the crew's steel or Kevlar helmets are welded to the upper edge of the turret.

The lower portion of the turret rear is visible when the bustle rack has been removed. Several threaded attachment points for the bustle rack screws are welded to the turret armor.

A .50-caliber ammunition can is stored on the right side of the turret, below the commander's cupola. It is held in place by strapping threaded through a pair of footman loops.

The commander's cupola sits on the right side of the turret. Bolted to the turret wall below the cupola is a pair of brackets for storing the .50-caliber M2 machine gun receiver. On the turret roof, forward of the cupola is the site housing for the gunner's XM44 periscope.

When prepared for an air drop, the .50-caliber machine gun is dismounted from its pintle and strapped to these brackets on the right side of the turret. Four footman loops are welded near the brackets and are used with the strapping that holds the .50-caliber machine gun in place.

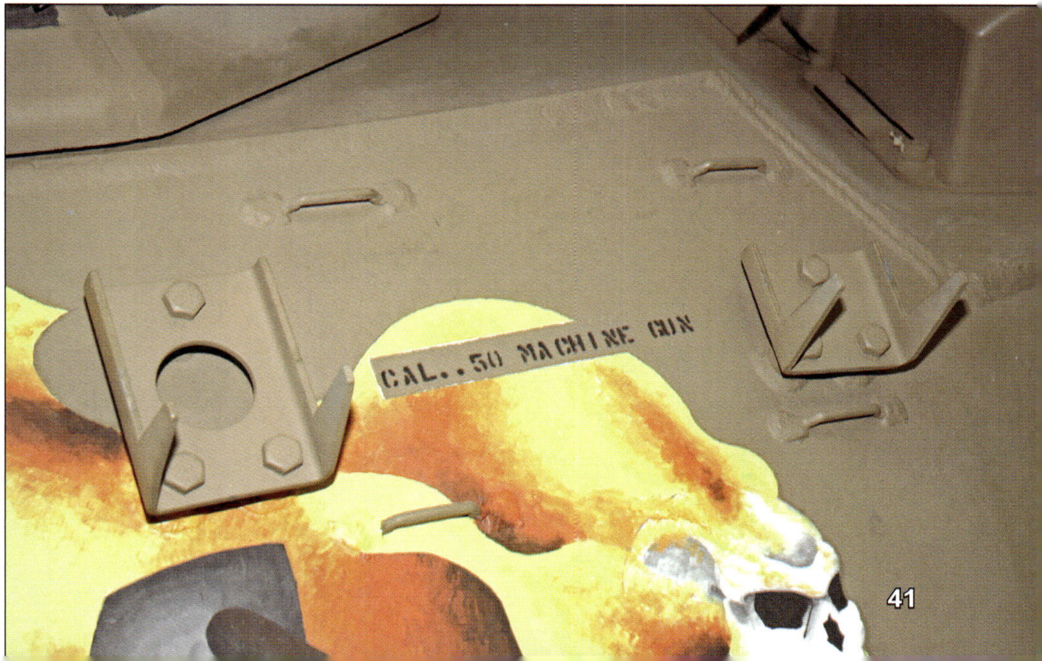

Each XM176 grenade launcher is loaded with an M34 White Phosphorous grenade and one M8 HC smoke grenade. Each launcher has a range of between 100 and 150 feet.

The optical transmitter box is bolted to the gun shield with eight hex-head bolts, four on each side of the box. The AN/VSS-3 searchlight is mounted on the left side of the gun shield. Stenciled on the top of the searchlight case is the warning "2 Man Lift."

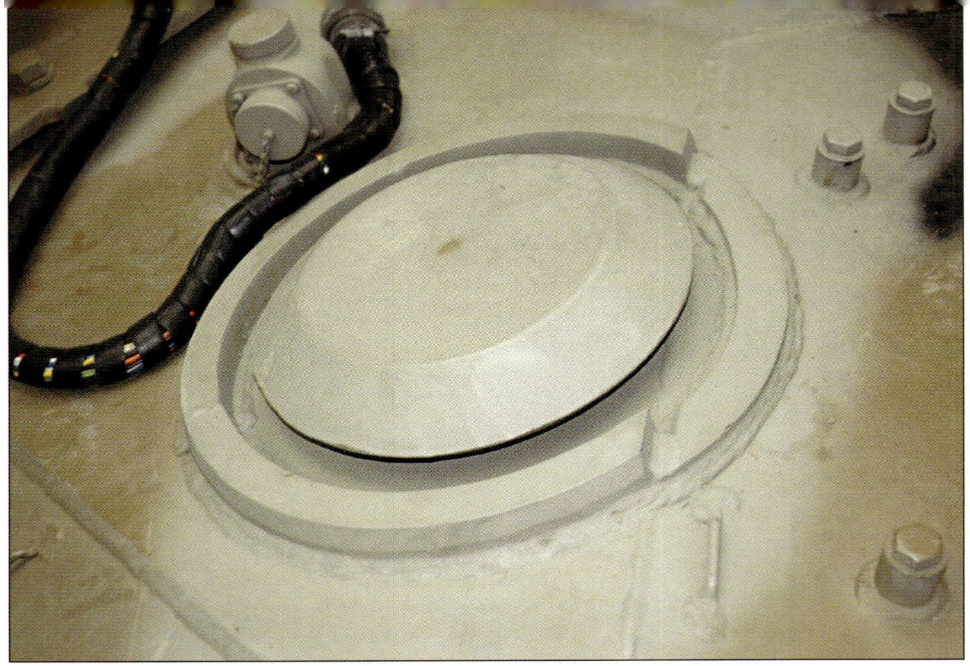

Early production Sheridans had the turret ventilator installed on the left, rear side wall of the turret. Later production M551s had the ventilator mounted on the left front of the turret roof.

The loader's hatch is located on the left side of the turret. In front of the loader's hatch is his M37 periscope.

The loader's M37 periscope can be traversed 360 degrees. The knob in front of the glass block locks the periscope cover down when the periscope has been lowered.

When closed, the loader's hatch cover is locked with a handle and pin mechanism. To lock it, the handle is raised and pushed forward. After the pin engages the hatch flange, the handle is lowered into the slot in the bracket.

A spring-loaded latch locks the loader's hatch in the open position. To disengage it, the loader pushes the latch backwards and pulls up on the hatch cover. An ammunition box for the commander's .50-caliber M2 machine gun is stored to the right of the latch.

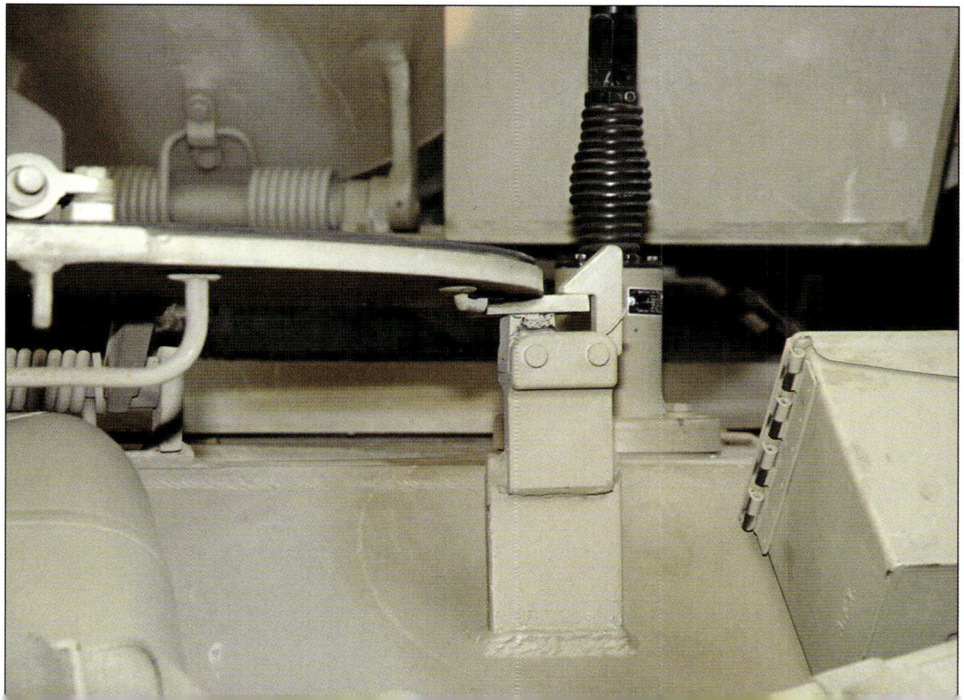

Bolted to the turret roof behind the loader's hatch is a radio antenna mount. The antenna itself extends upwards from the mount about nine feet.

A housing on the right front of the turret roof covers the gunner's XM44 periscope. The XM44 and its later E1 and E2 versions is the gunner's primary sight for night time operations. A ballistic cover, which the gunner opens from inside the turret, protects the periscope lens.

A series of clamps and screws secure each vision block to the cupola. Each block can be replaced by pushing it out from the cupola after removing the clamps and screws. Above the blocks is a hinge for one of the split hatch covers.

The cupola is fitted with 10 ballistic glass vision blocks. With the hatches closed, the vision blocks provide the commander with 360 degree vision around the tank.

On the M551A1, the vision block below the commander's machine gun pintle was replaced by the AN/VVG-1 laser range finder. Components boxes for the laser range finder were fitted inside the rear of the commander's armor enclosure. (Brent Sauer)

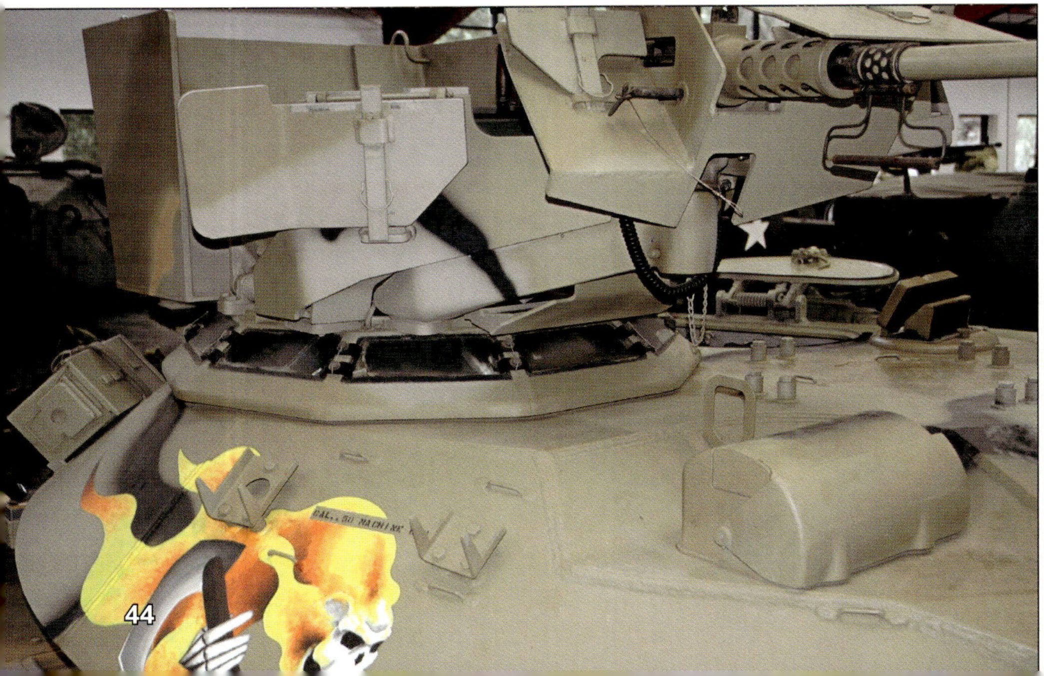

When initially deployed, the design of the .50-caliber M2 machine gun pintle mount forced the vehicle commander to be exposed at the front and rear, from the waist up when using the weapon. The open cupola split hatches did provide some protection to his sides. Protection for the exposed commander was made possible with the addition of a ballistic shield kit that was retrofitted to the cupola.

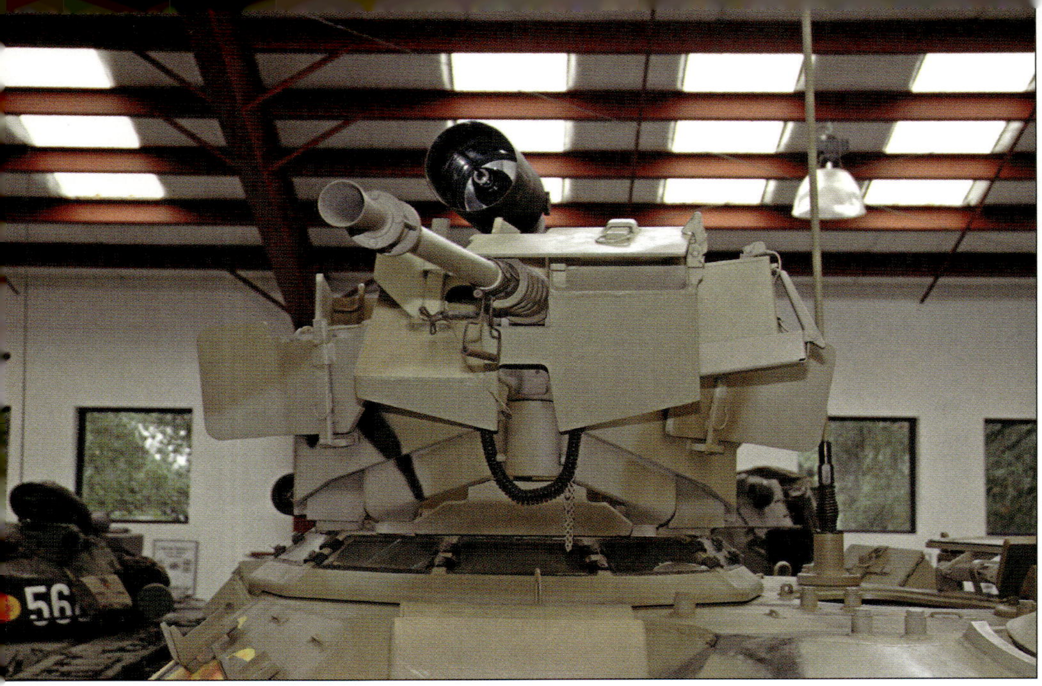

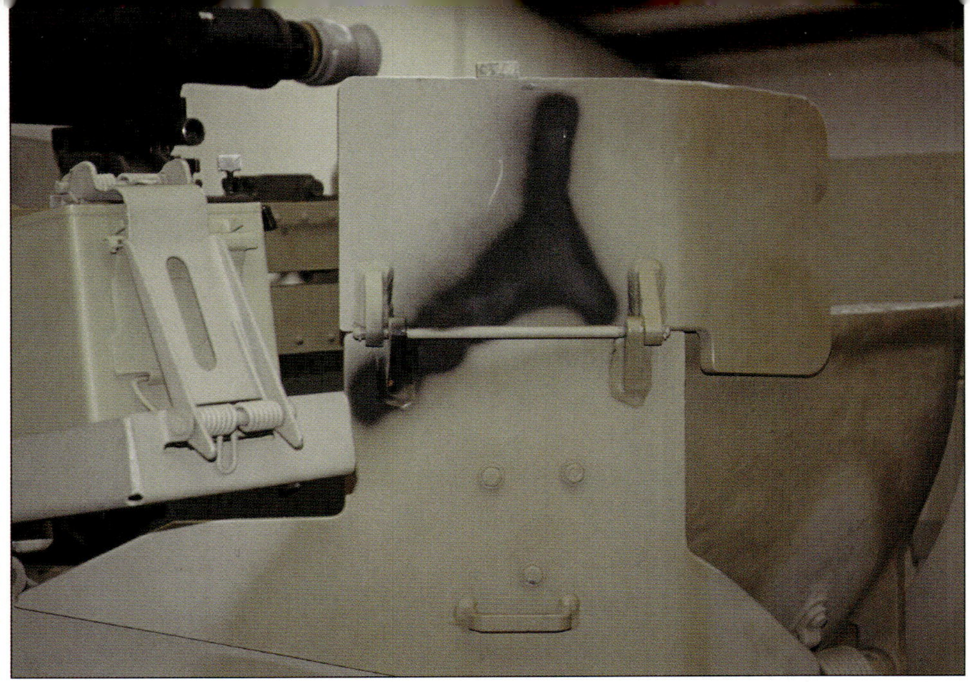

Near all around protection is provided to the commander by the ballistic shield kit. A flash suppressor is mounted on the end of the machine gun barrel.

Both the left- and right-side ballistic shields are hinged in the center and fold downwards when not in use.

The ammunition box and tray are located behind the front shield assembly. When removing or installing the box and tray, the shield could be in either the upright or folded forward position.

When the top half of the ballistic shield is folded down, the shield bar lock slides into a bracket on the lower half of the shield. The lock prevents the upper half from bouncing around while the vehicle is in motion.

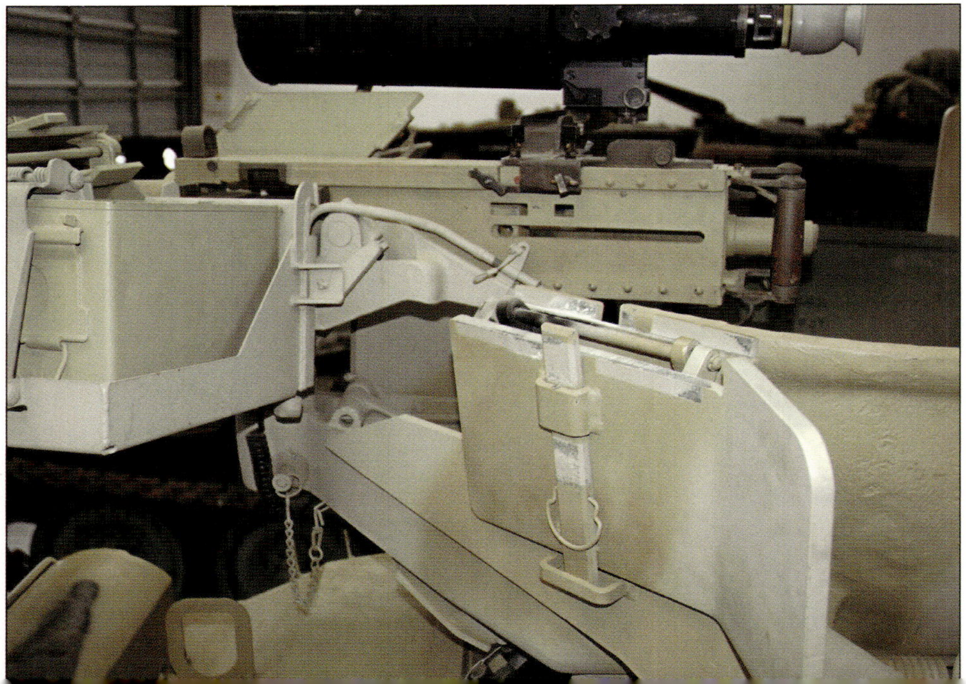

The cupola hatch covers provide additional protection for the commander when they are opened. A ballistic enclosure is fitted to the rear of the cupola.

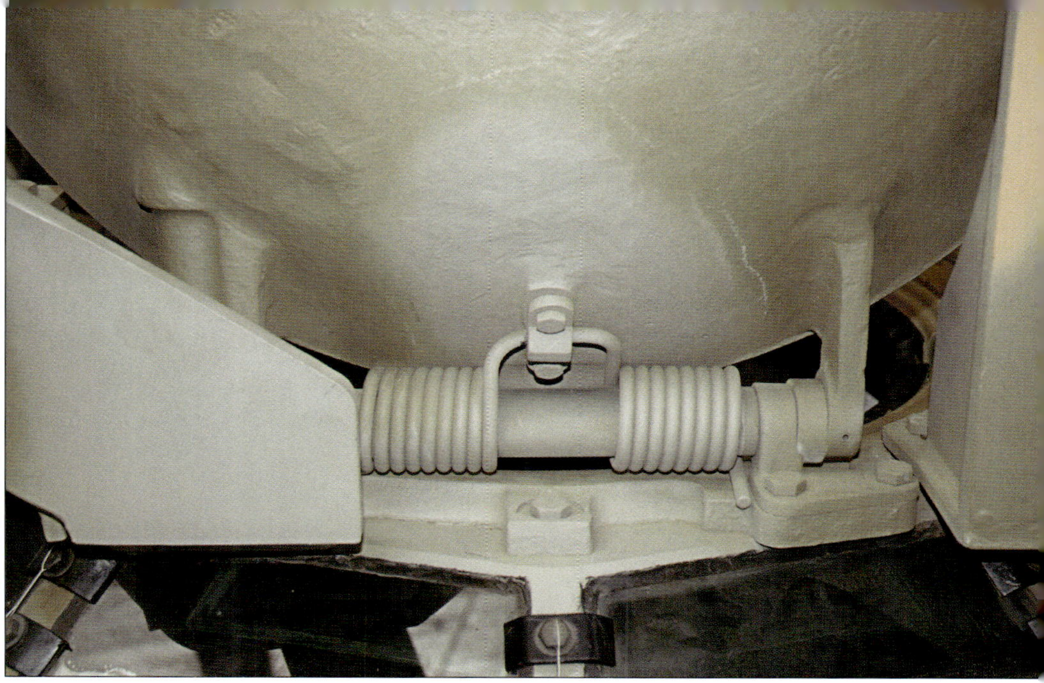

The cupola hatch covers are hinged at the bottom. The ballistic shield assembly is attached to brackets on both sides of the hatch cover.

By using the protection provided by the raised cupola hatch covers, additional armor shields are not needed to protect the sides of the commander's position.

Seen from the rear, the commander's ballistic enclosure has a folding door that opens outwards. A pair of latches at the top of the enclosure keep it closed.

The right side shield assembly is folded down in this view. The opened cupola hatch fills in the space between the forward and rear armor assemblies. Due to its size and shape, Sheridan crewmembers referred to the shield assembly as the "bird cage." Off to the right and in front of the cupola is the gunner's XM44 periscope housing.

For night firing and observation, the M2 machine gun could have an AN/TVS-2 night vision sight attached to it. The AN/TVS-2 amplifies available star and moon light and intensifies it within the scope so the user can see objects in the dark.

A locking bar attached to the inner face locks the shield in either open or closed position. "U" shaped brackets welded to the shield faces hold the locking bars in place.

The AN/TVS-2 is mounted on a bracket that is screwed to the top of the M2's receiver. The large knob on the side controls objective focus while the eyepiece controls focus on the image intensifier output window.

The right side shield assembly is folded down in this view. The opened cupola hatch fills in the space between the forward and rear armor assemblies. Due to its size and shape, Sheridan crew members referred to the shield assembly as the "bird cage."

The .50-caliber M2 machine gun and pintle are mounted on a pintle support that is bolted to the cupola. Ammunition for the weapon is supplied by a box with a capacity of 105 belted rounds.

The pintle support is attached to the cupola with four hex-head screws. The bottom protective cover plate fills the open space between the pintle support legs. Protruding down from the bottom of the M2 is the machine gun travel lock lever.

Hatch cover release levers are located on each hatch. The hatches can be opened or closed by pulling down on the ring, which releases the locking pin. Two hatch locking levers are located on the left hatch cover and are used to lock both hatches closed.

Cast into the insides of both of the cupola hatch covers are foundry logos and part numbers.

The dome shape of the hatch covers is clearly evident when they are closed. Also clear is the gap between the front ballistic shield pieces and the rear ballistic enclosure. This gap in the commander's protection is filled when the hatch covers are locked open.

A pair of 105-round ammunition boxes for the .50-caliber machine gun are stored in the ballistic enclosure and allow the commander quick access to extra ammunition when the box mounted on the gun runs out.

Seen from the front, the bottom protective cover minimizes the open space below the pintle mount that would otherwise allow enemy fire to hit the commander.

The laser range finder (LRF) replaced the forward vision block in the cupola. A power cable protected by an armored cover ran from the right side of the LRF housing to an electronics box in the rear of the commander's ballistic enclosure. A battery box for the LRF was also installed in the rear of the enclosure. (Roy Lingle)

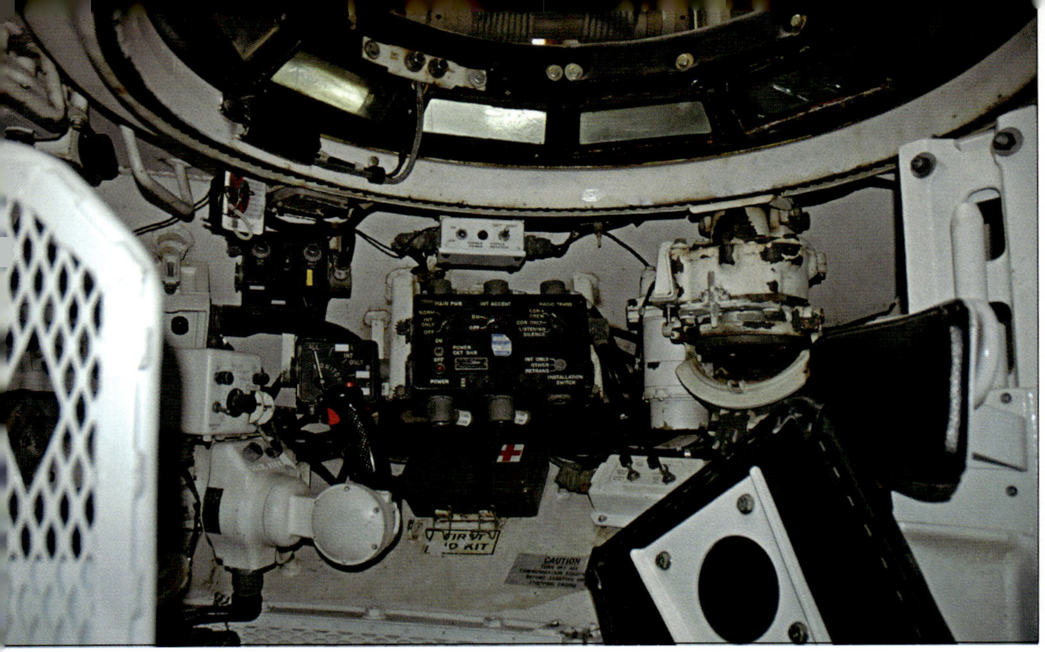

Most of the turret controls are located on the right side of the turret with the commander and gunner. The olive drab box in the center is the AM-1780/VRC master control unit for the M551's radio and intercom systems. Below it is a small first aid kit. The black handle on the left is the commander's power control handle. The commander's folding seat is in the foreground.

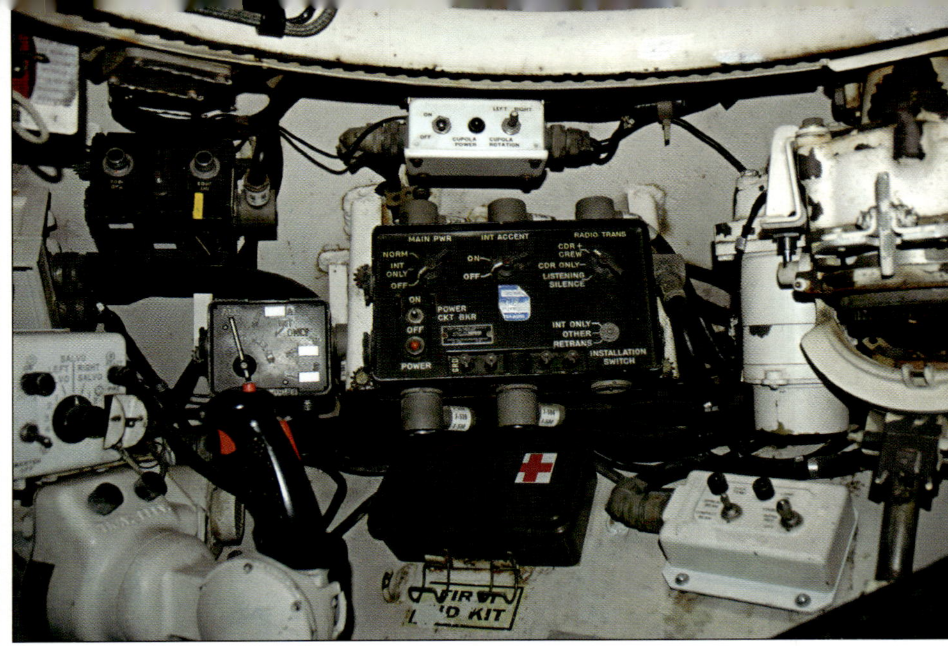

The AM-1780/VRC is the master control for the M551's radio and intercom systems. Settings on it can allow the entire crew to transmit on the receiver/transmitter, or can restrict transmission to the commander only. A listening silence setting is also provided wherein no transmissions take place, but incoming messages can be received.

Located above the AM-1780/VRC is the cupola control box. Switches on this box allow the commander to electrically rotate the cupola.

In the M551, manual traversing of the cupola is accomplished with a ratchet mechanism. By extending the handle outwards, the commander can traverse the cupola by ratcheting the handle in the direction he wants the cupola to rotate.

The 10 ballistic glass blocks in the cupola provide the commander with 360-degree vision when buttoned up.

On the M551A1, the center ballistic glass block in the cupola was replaced by the AN/VVG-1 LRF. The two tan colored domes in the center of the unit are range and reset lamps. The black knob on the lower right of the unit is the azimuth control while the knob on the left side is the elevation control.

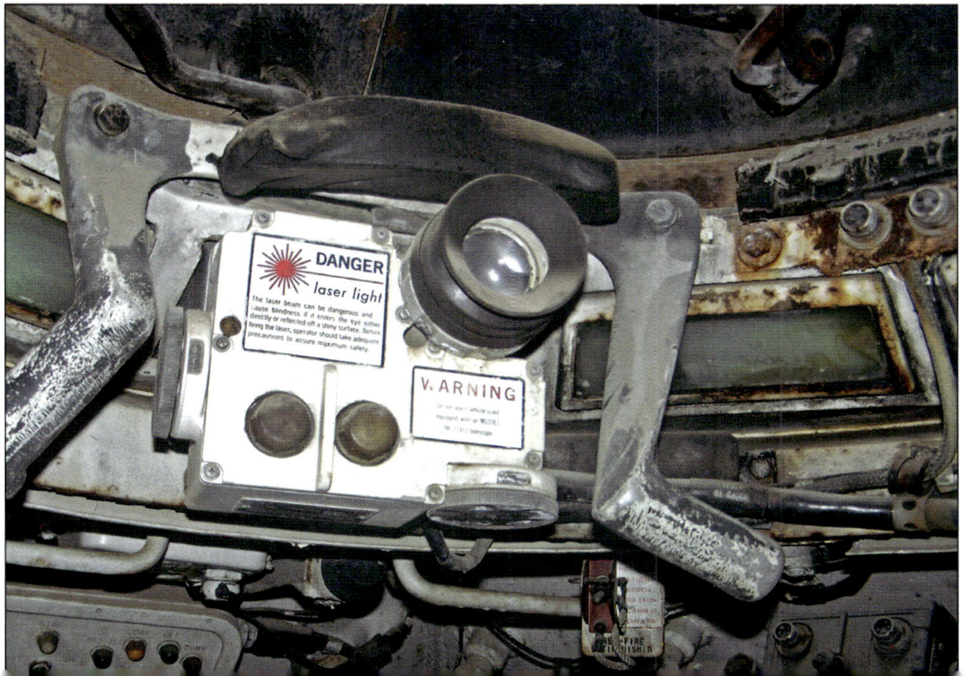

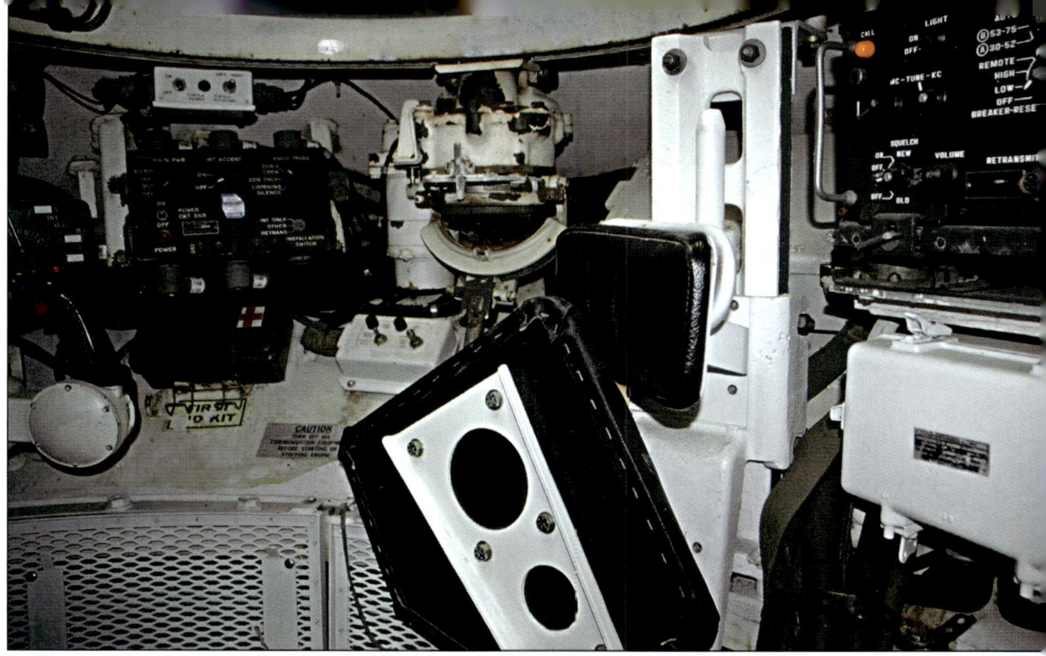

The commander's seat is spring loaded and folds up against its mounting bracket when not in use. Its height can be adjusted by pulling up on the adjustment lever located next to the back rest.

Wire grilles make up the sides of the turret basket. In cold weather operations, they can be covered to keep cold air from entering the crew compartment through the engine compartment bulkhead.

Below the commander's seat is the elevated turret sub-floor. This platform allowed the commander to stand up in the turret and use the cupola vision blocks. The platform itself is bolted to the floor of the turret basket.

The commander can operate the turret and armament via his power control handle. The two black knobs in front of the handle are used to adjust the traverse trim of the turret and elevation trim of the gun mount. A palm switch on the handle acts like a safety and when depressed allows the commander to traverse the turret or elevate/depress the main gun. The switch box in front of the handle controls the smoke grenade launchers.

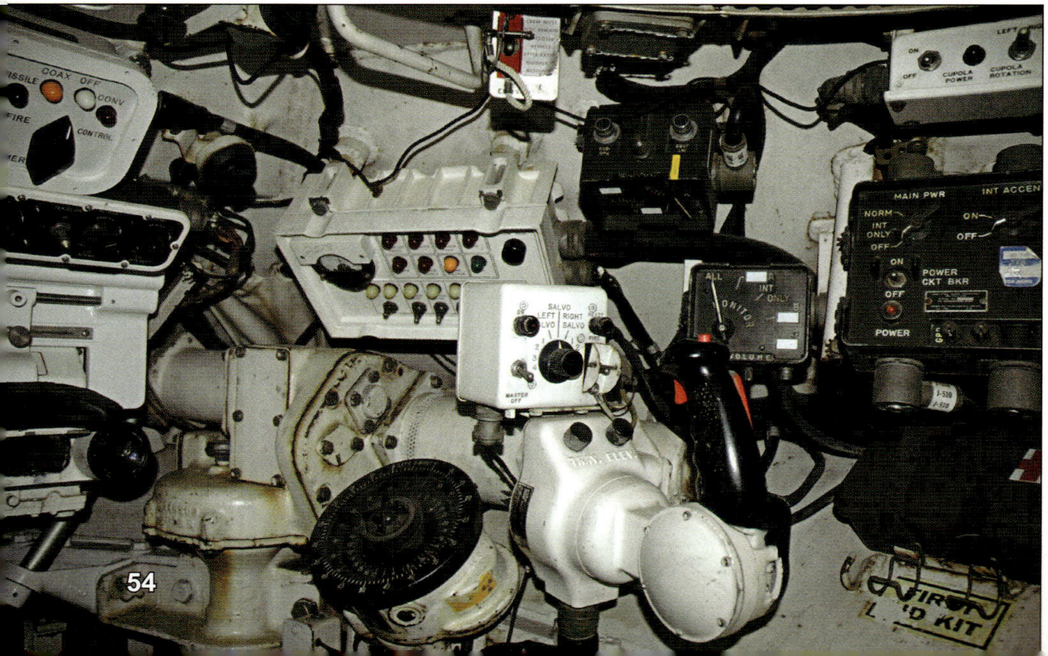

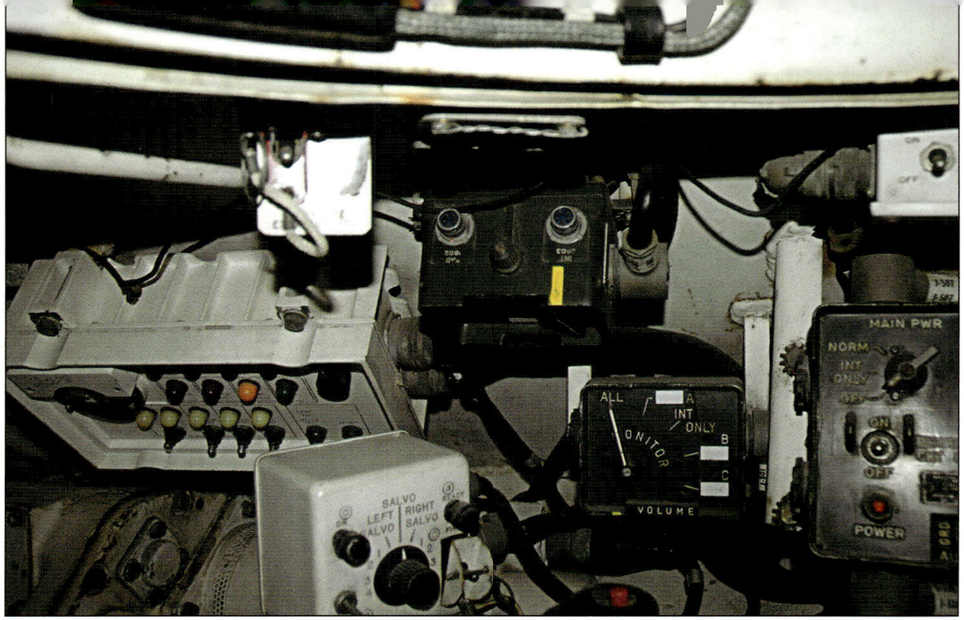

Two C-2298/VRC intercom control boxes are located to the left of the AM-1780/VRC. The commander uses the box on top while the one below it is for the gunner. Each crew member plugs his CVC helmet into his assigned box in order to communicate within the tank or with others outside of it.

Seen here are most of the gunner's controls. The sight on the left is the M127 telescope. It is flanked on the right by the XM44 gunner's periscope. Above them are various switch panels for the turret and gun. The black disc on the far right is the turret azimuth indicator.

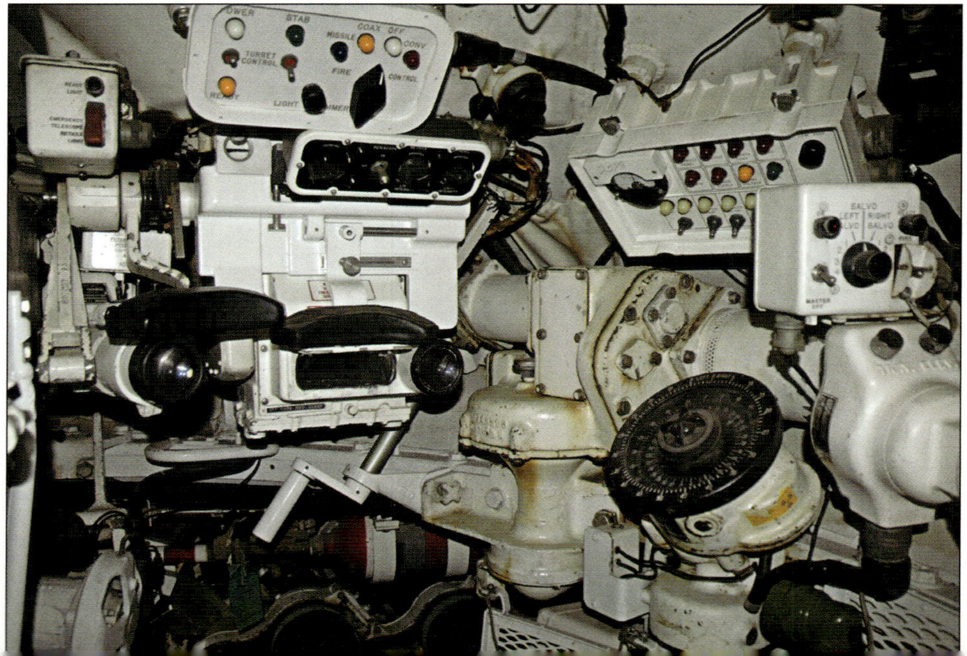

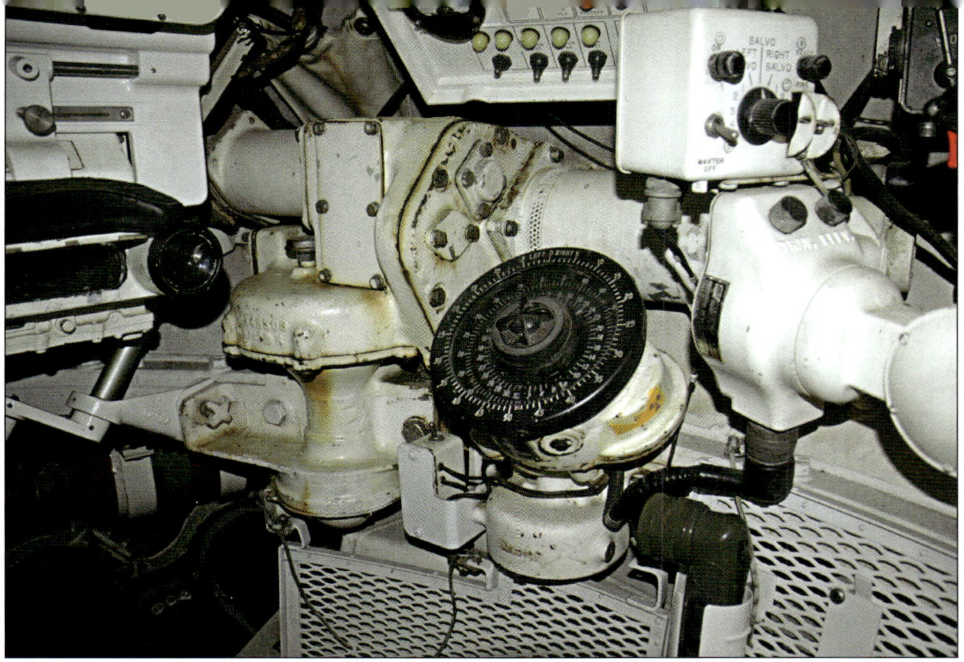

The azimuth indicator is used to measure the deflection angle of the gun-launcher. It is located on the right side of the gunner, in front of the commander's power control handle.

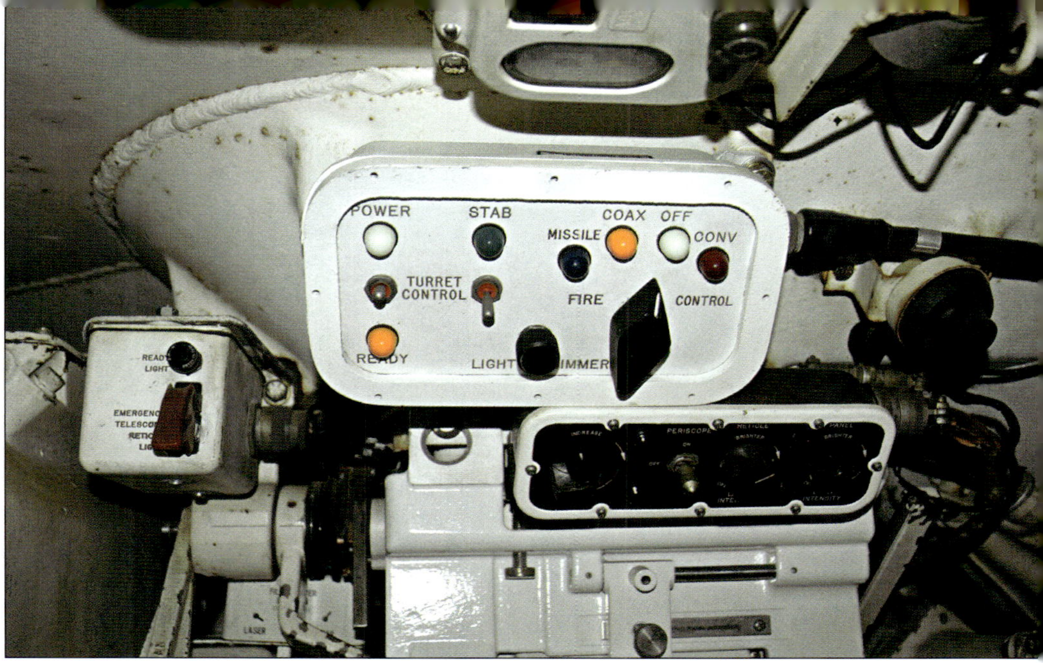

The toggle switch on the far left side of the panel powers the turret on when positioned upwards. Next to it is the turret stabilizer switch. The large black knob is the fire control selector and has settings for firing the missile, co-axial machine gun, off and conventional ammunition.

The gunner is provided with two sighting systems, the M127 telescope on the left and the XM44 periscope on the right. Directly above the XM44 is the periscope control panel. The large box above it is the gun and turret control selector panel.

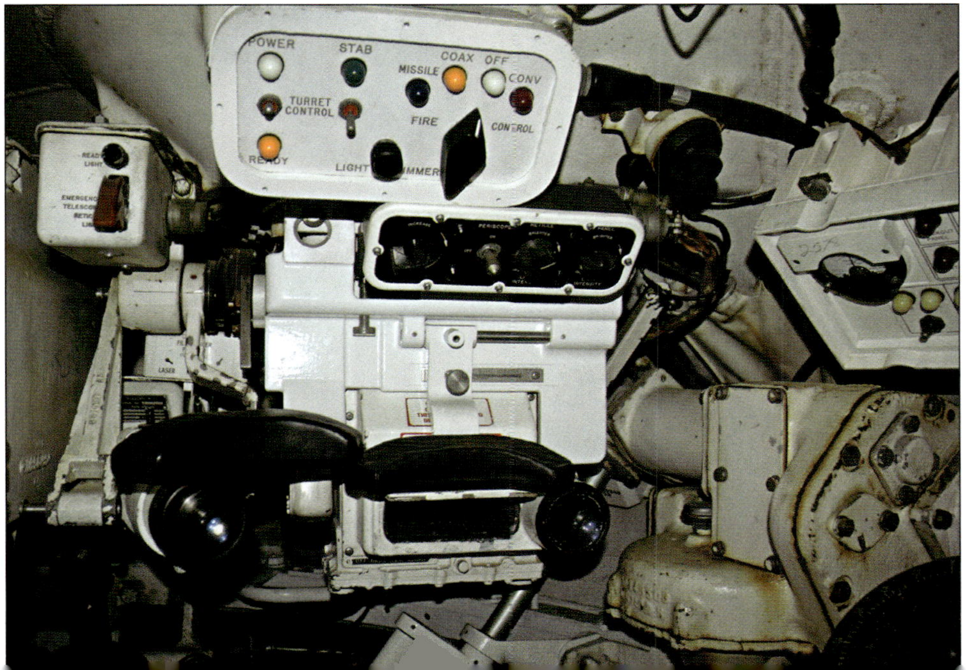

An emergency power switch for the M127 telescope is located to the left of the turret control panel. The red cover is normally safety wired to the box.

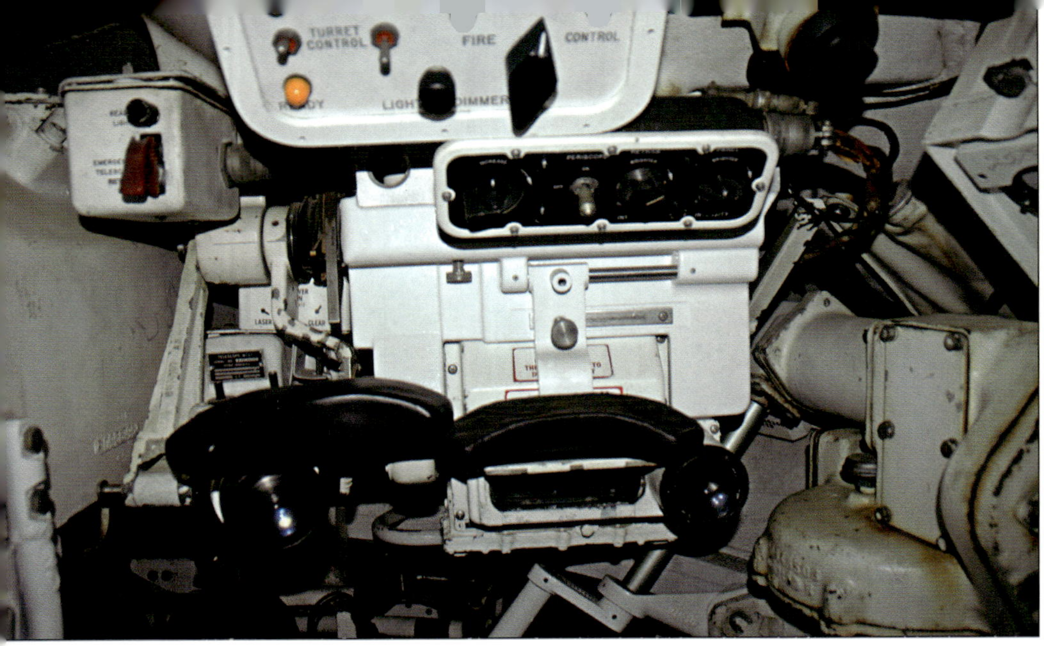

The M127 telescope is the primary day sight for the gunner while the XM44 is the primary night sight. A handle used for opening the external ballistic cover for the sight housing is located on the right side of the XM44 unit.

The gunner uses the view window during the day for target scanning. The actual gunsight reticles can be viewed using the eyepiece on the sight. The brow pad above the view window can be adjusted to the left or right depending upon which sight the gunner is using. Loosening the silver knob on the brow-pad bracket and sliding the bracket in the direction required accomplish adjustment.

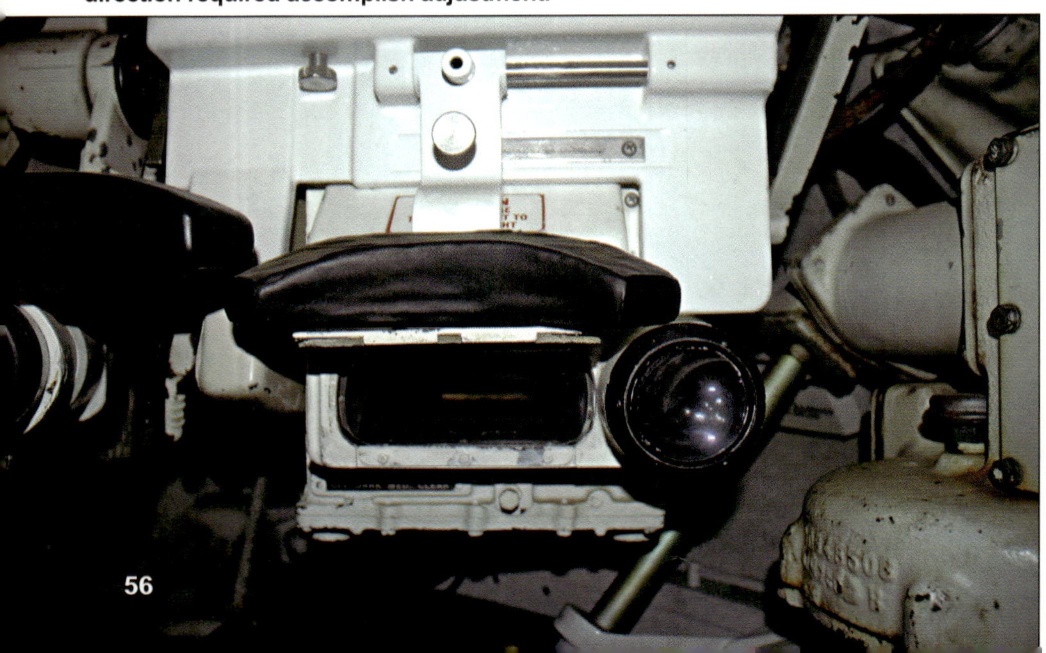

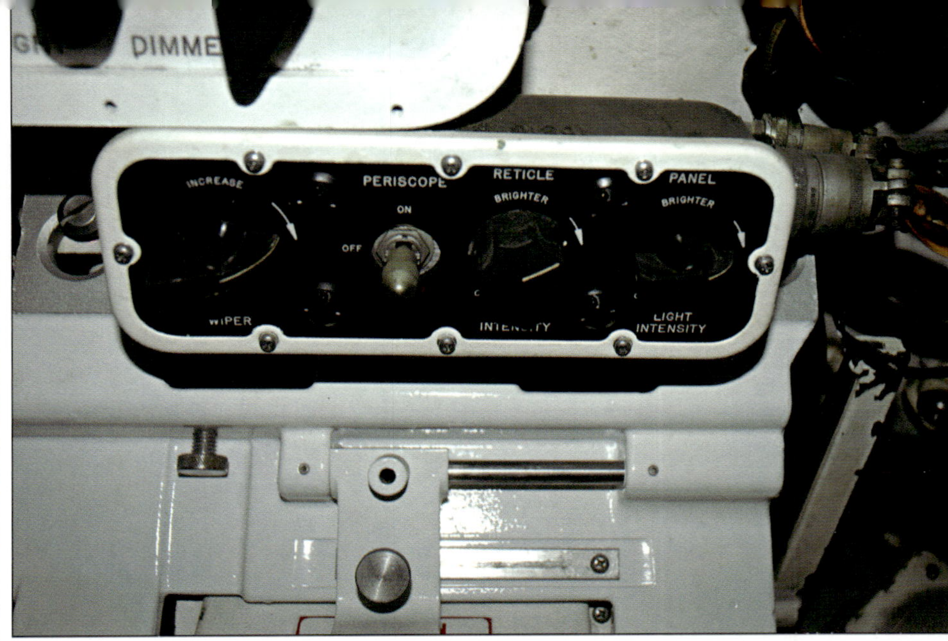

The control panel for the XM44 is above the periscope. The knob on the left is for the periscope window wiper. The toggle switch illuminates the reticles for night operations. Two control-panel lights are mounted between the window-wiper knob and power toggle switch. Two more panel lights are located between the reticle-intensity and panel-light-intensity knobs. The reticle knob adjusts the light intensity of the reticle while the panel-light knob adjusts the intensity of the panel lights.

The primary day sight is the M127 gunner's telescope, which can be set to either 8- or 12-power magnification. Just above the eyepiece is a brow pad for the gunner's head.

Viewed from the commander's position, more of the gunner's position is visible. The white disc with a metal handle on the left is the manual elevation handwheel. Just below it is the gunner's power-control handle with the manual traversing handle on the upper right.

To traverse the turret, the gunner grabs the handle and presses the palm switch on the handle's side to the left or to the right, depending on which direction he wants the turret to move. To elevate or depress the gun mount, the same sort of procedure is followed except that the handle is pushed forward to depress the gun or pulled backwards to elevate it.

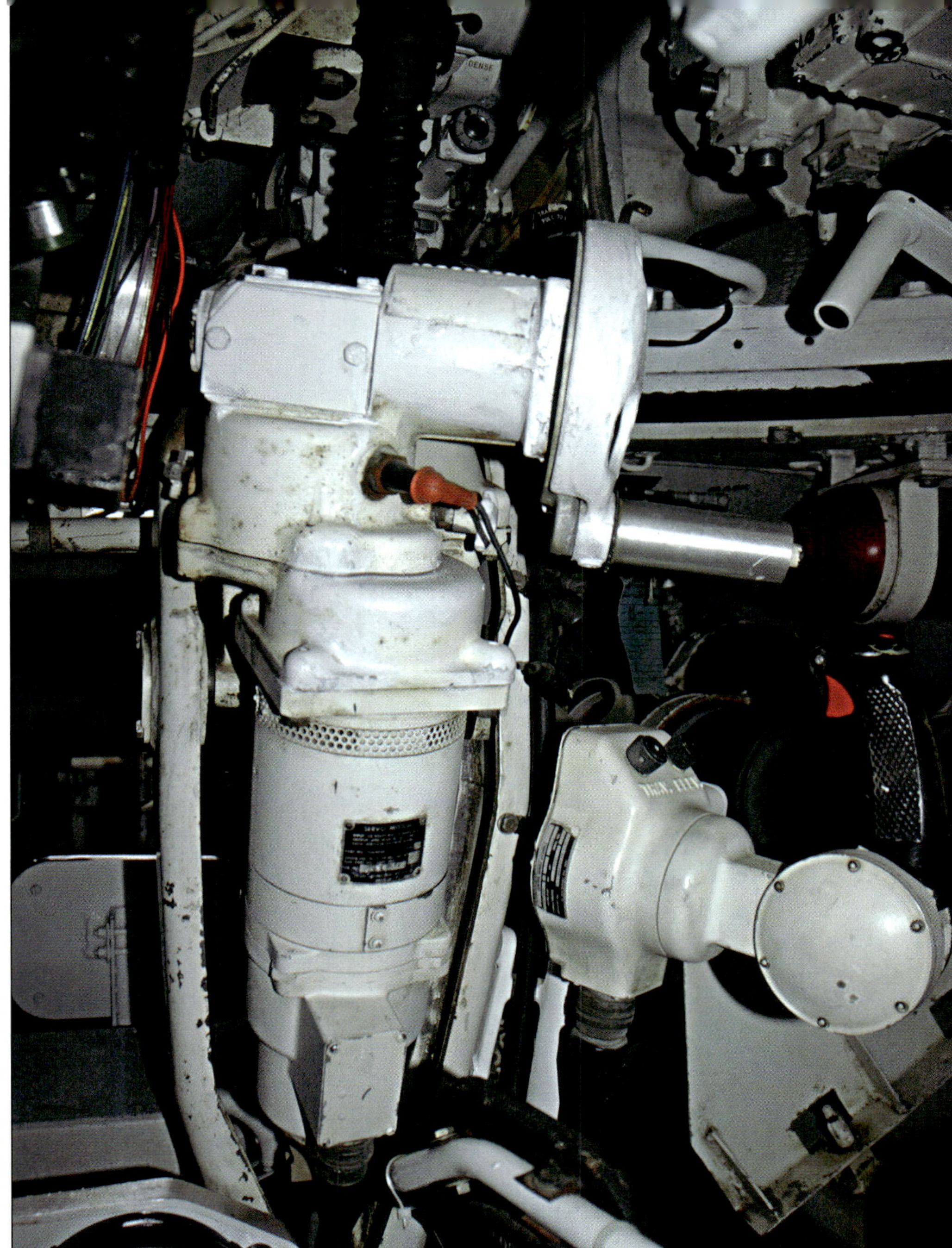

The elevating mechanism servo motor is located next to the gunner's control handle. Above it is the manual elevation handwheel. On the tip of the handwheel is a firing button for the main and co-axial weapons.

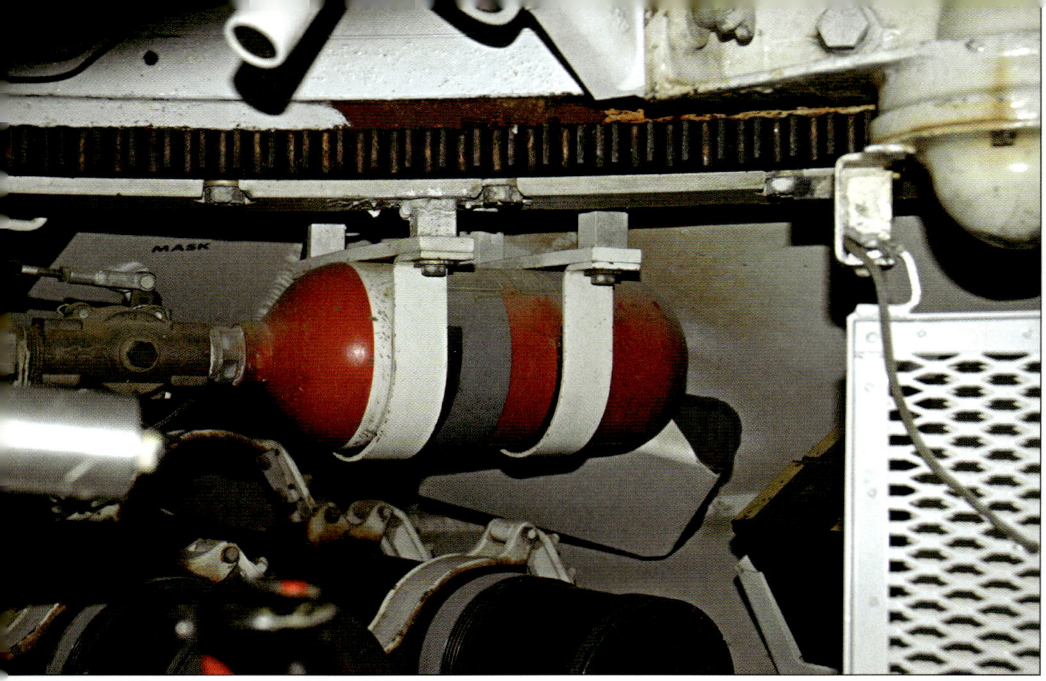

A fire-extinguisher bottle is mounted on the ceiling of the crew compartment just in front of the gunner's position. It can be activated via a handle on the outside of the hull or with switches in the driver's compartment and at the commander's station.

The manual traversing handle is located on the right side of the turret, next to the gunner.

The ammunition racks next to the driver are accessible to the loader when the turret is turned to approximately the 3 o'clock position.

A pair of 200-round ammunition boxes are stowed in the right side of the hull behind the right side main gun ammunition racks. Like the main gun rounds, they are accessible when the turret is in the 3-o'clock position.

The gunner's seat is located in front of the subfloor. The backrest can be removed to allow easier access or egress to and from the seat. The seat itself can be adjusted both vertically and horizontally using a pair of adjustment handles on the seat mount.

A small pad for the gunner's leg is mounted on a support brace that runs from near the elevation motor to the subfloor. The gunner's seat vertical adjustment "T" handle can be seen just in front of the canteen.

The large breech of the 152mm gun-launcher M81 is seen opened. The grey knobbed breech actuator handle is used to open and close the breech chamber above it.

The breech chamber opens out and to the left. When the breech is opened, a loading tray extends upwards from below the bore and rests at the bore's opening to assist the loader in chambering a round.

The tray has a slot or "keyway" to ensure the missiles are properly oriented when they are inserted into the bore.

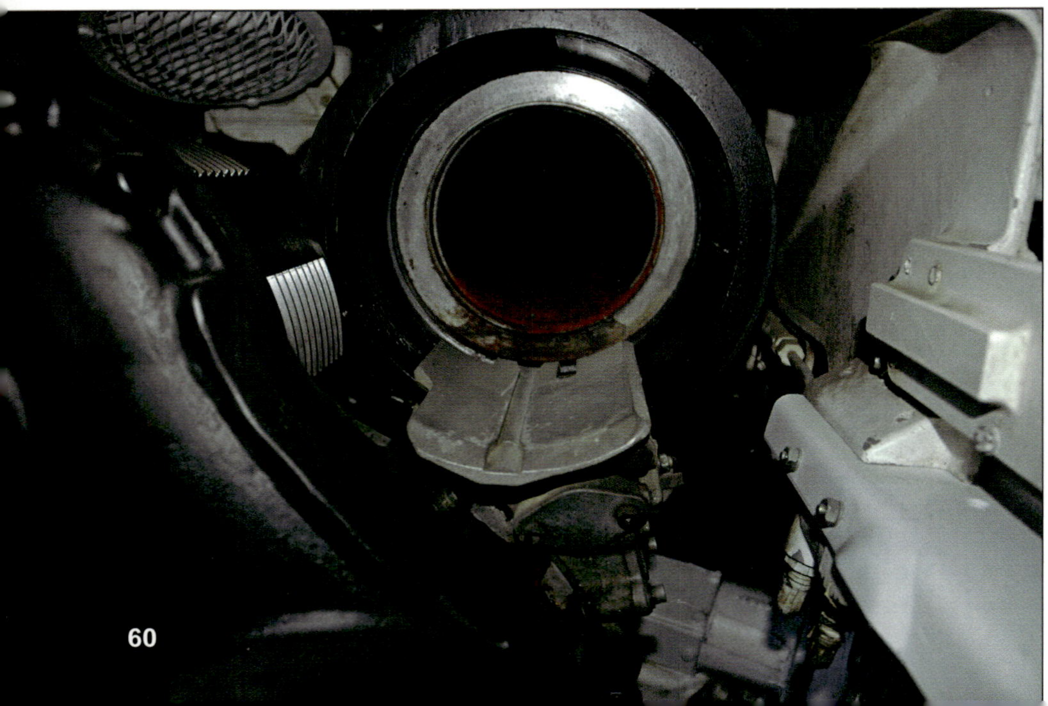

As the missile is slid down the loading tray, the key on the missile engages the "keyway" inside the barrel. Unlike the rifling grooves, the keyway does not twist through the length of the barrel bore.

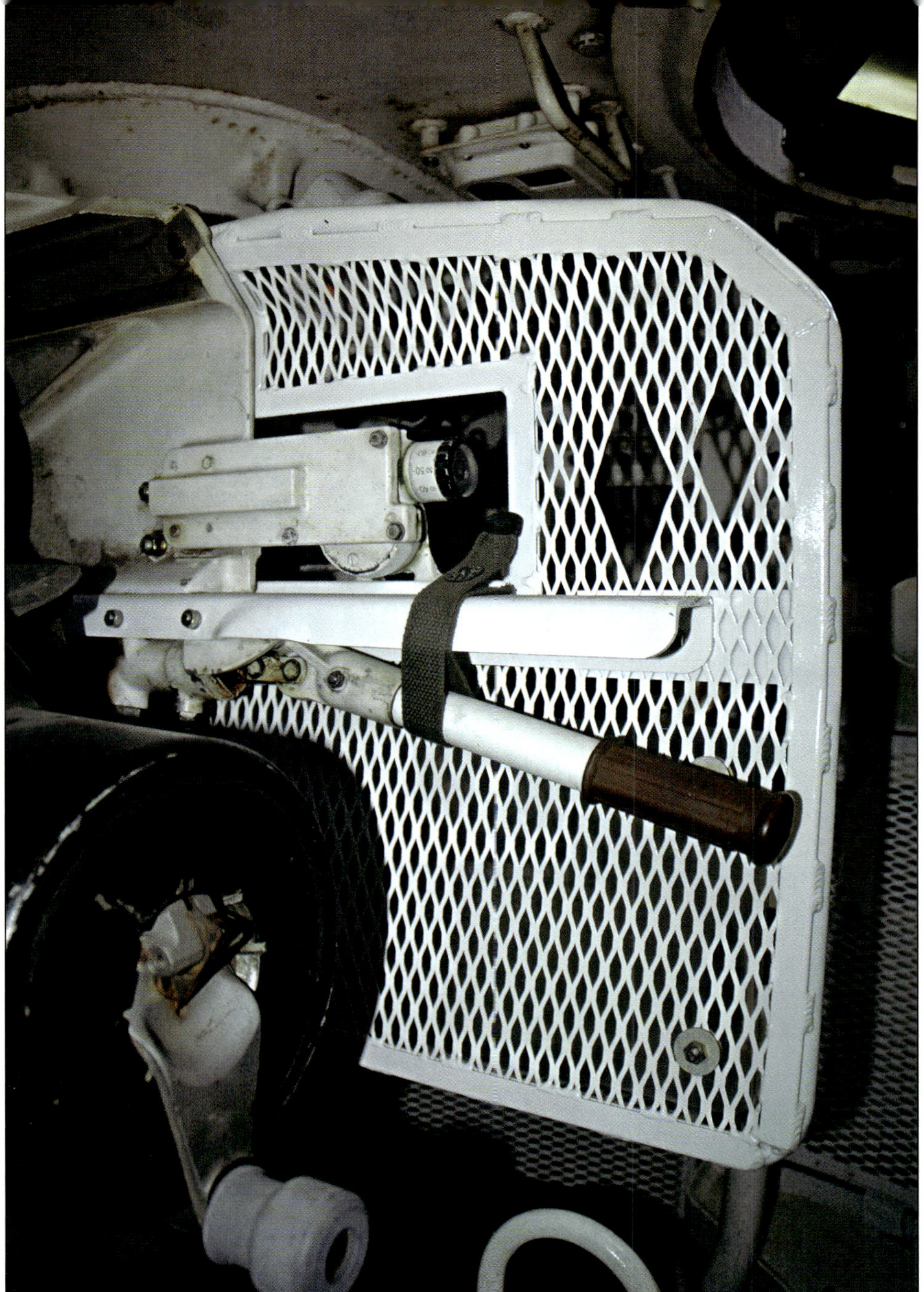

A metal recoil guard is located on the right side of the breech assembly. The handle strapped to the guard is the recoil mechanism hand pump. Above it is the M13A1C elevation quadrant. The M13A1C is used to measure elevation/depression.

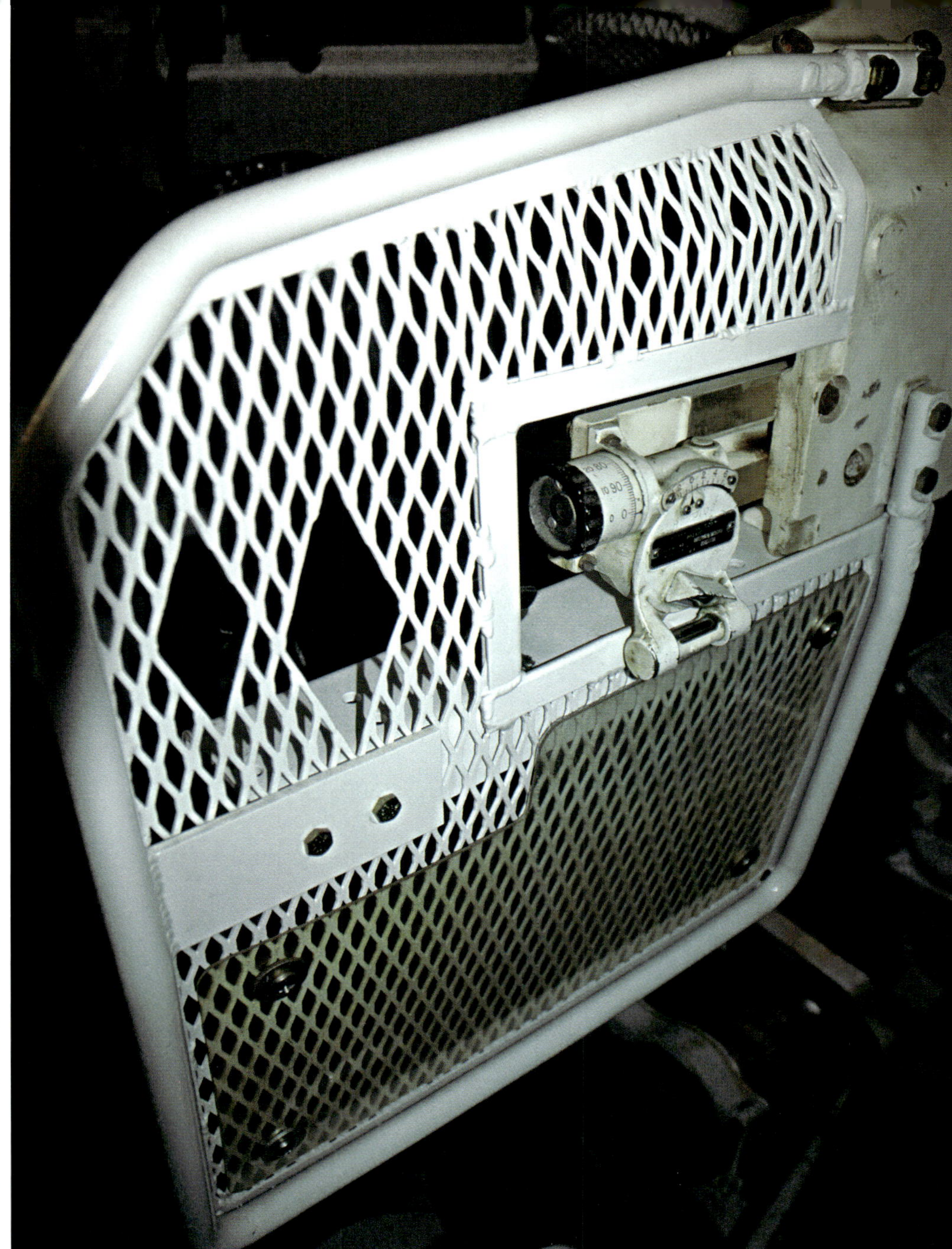

Viewed here from the the gunner's position, M13A1 is used while engaging targets in the indirect fire mode. Turning the black micrometer knob counterclockwise elevates the gun from zero elevation while a clockwise turn depresses the gun from zero.

The breech actuator handle has two settings, manual and electric. When the small pin in the center is flipped downwards as seen here, it is set to be manually opened. When flipped upwards, it could be opened electrically using a toggle switch on the loader's control box.

A 7.62mm M73 or M219 machine gun is normally mounted co-axially with the 152mm M81 gun-launcher. Its primary purpose is to engage infantry and other targets not suitable for the main armament. The barrel jacket is clamped into the circular bracket while the muzzle is inserted in the gun shield behind it. A chute for spent brass is on the right near the breech.

Seen on the left is a High Explosive-Tracer (HE-T) XM657E2 shell. The XM657E2 projectile weighed 43.1 lbs (19.6kg) with the complete round weighing 50 lbs (22.7kg). On the right is the MGM-51C Shillelagh missile. As fired, the missile weighed 61.5 lbs (28kg).

A bag for spent brass is attached to a frame that hangs below the spent brass chute.

The turret ventilator extracts toxic fumes from the turret that can build up while the weapons are being fired. A toggle switch is used by the loader to turn the fan off or on as needed.

The front of the loader's position is a busy place where many components are fitted. On the left is the loader's M37 periscope. The control box for the AN/VSS-3 searchlight is in the center with one of the turret dome lights bolted to the ceiling in front of it. On the right is the turret ventilator.

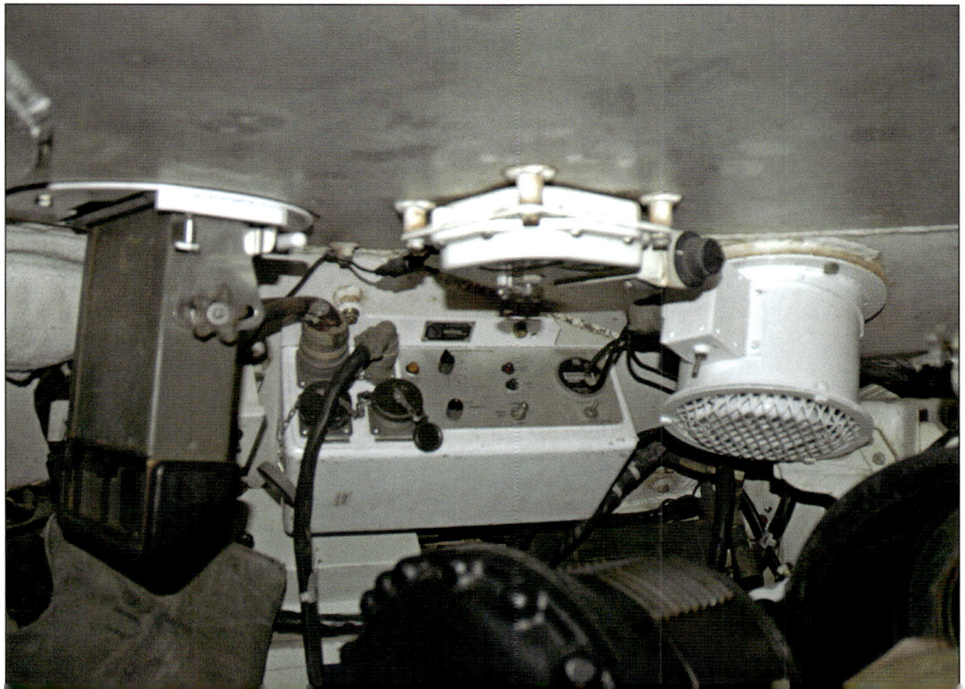

Interior lighting for the turret is provided by a pair of dome lights. This light is mounted over the loader's position. Both red and white light lenses are provided.

A M37 periscope allows the loader to see outside of the tank when it is closed up. A star shaped knob on the right and the adjusting screw above it are used to tilt the periscope for best viewing.

The AN/VSS-3 searchlight control box is seen here in front of the loader's position. The black knob below the data plate is the circuit test switch. Below it is the local/remote switch that is used to select where the light will be operated from. The center toggle switch was used to power the light on in visible or infrared mode while the toggle switch on the far right sets the width of the light beam.

To clean out residue left inside the bore by the combustible case ammunition, a closed breech scavenging system (CBSS) is used. The CBSS comprises a four-stage air compressor, two compressed-air cylinders, a pressure gauge, a regulator, and various hoses and fittings. When activated, the CVSS blows air into the bore and removes most if not all residue from fired combustible case cartridges. The red handle opens and closes the air shutoff valve for the system.

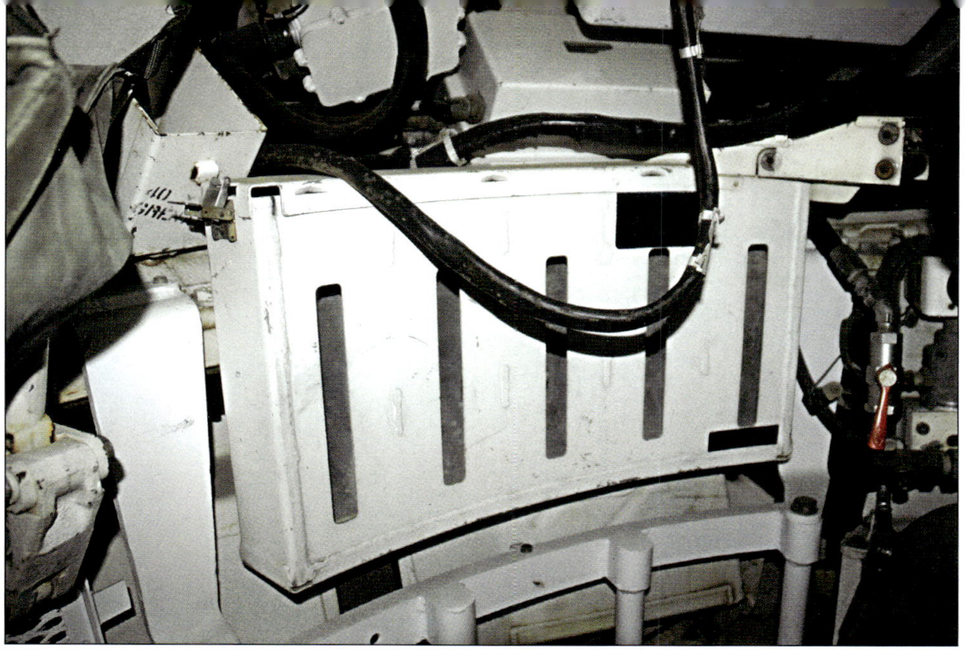

The ready ammunition box for the co-axial machine gun is mounted on the turret ring below the searchlight control box. The box is divided into five compartments internally and is loaded from right to left.

A three-round ready rack is on the left side of the turret, next to the loader. It can hold missiles or conventional rounds. Rubber pads are affixed to the racks to provide cushioning for the rounds.

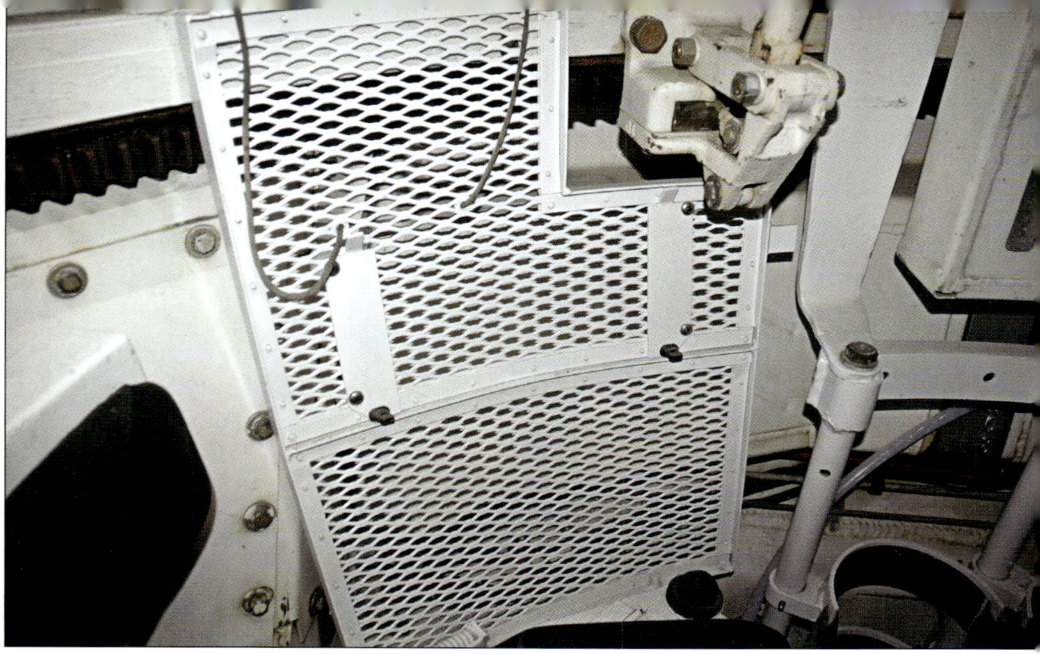

Grille work is bolted to the turret ring and floor. It forms the sides of the turret basket and helps protect the loader from being caught by interior vehicle parts when the turret is traversing. The turret traverse lock is on the right of the grille.

When the handle of the turret traverse lock is pulled backwards, it locks into the released position. To lock the turret and prevent it from traversing, the handle is pushed down and forwards.

Like the commander's, the loader's seat is spring loaded with the seat being held down by the weight of the loader.

Unlike the other seats in the M551, the loader's seat is not adjustable. The loader's backrest is mounted on a bracket that is bolted to the turret ring. Below the seat is the oddment stowage box.

The oddment stowage box is a place for the crew to carry miscellaneous parts, tools and equipment that may not otherwise have a standardized stowage place.

Beneath the loader's seat and oddment stowage box is the air compress for the CBSS. The vertical cylinder in front of the compressor houses an air cartridge filter for the compressor unit.

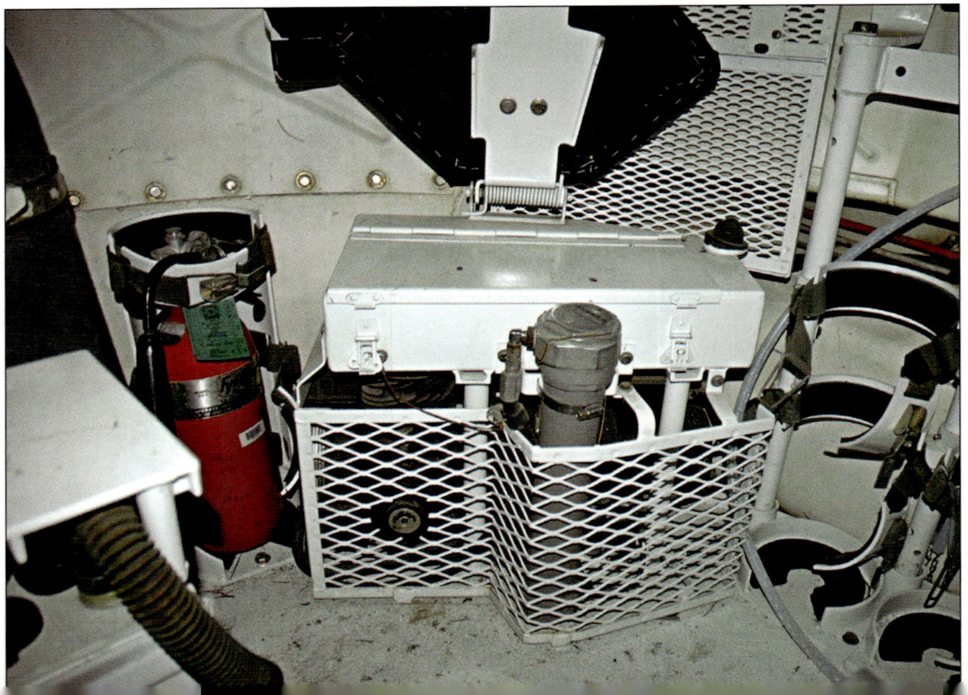

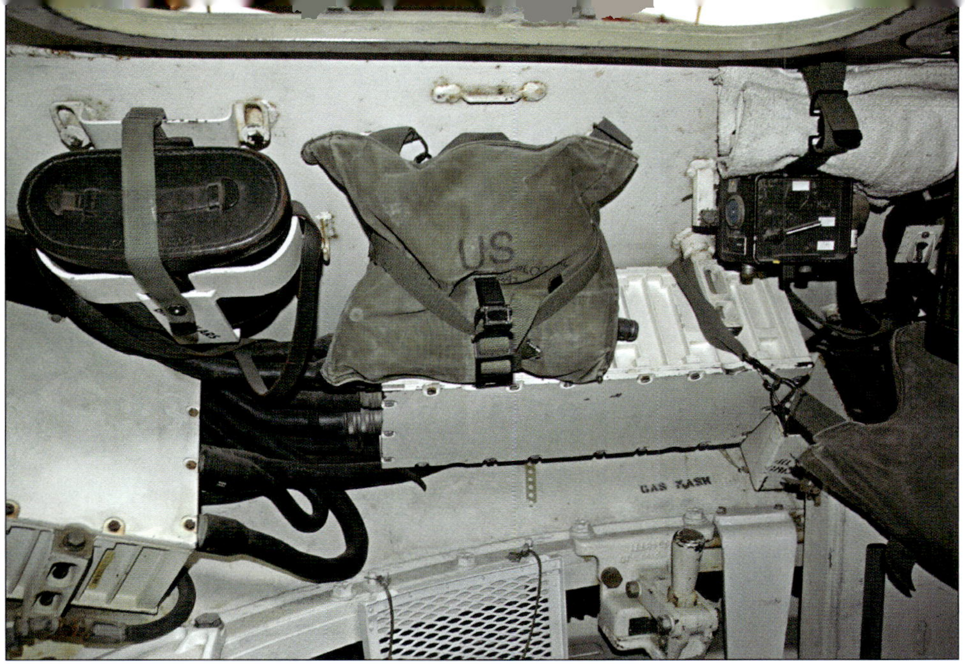

A binocular case is stored near the loader. Next to it is an M25A1 protective mask carrier. The two white boxes with the numerous cables extending out from them are the modulator (on the left) and the signal data convertor (on the right). They are part of the guidance system for the Shillelagh missile.

The loader's C-2298/VRC intercom set allows him to communicate with the rest of the crew or with others outside of the tank.

Output from the signal-data convertor on the right is converted to high current by the modulator. The high current is needed to operate the transmitter that is positioned above the gun shield. The red "T" handled item is the blasting machine. The loader uses it to fire the 152mm gun-launcher in an emergency, such as a hang-fire.

In the rear of the turret, between the commander and loader, is the vehicle's radio set. It consists of an RT-246/VRC transmitter (on the left) and an R-442/VRC receiver.

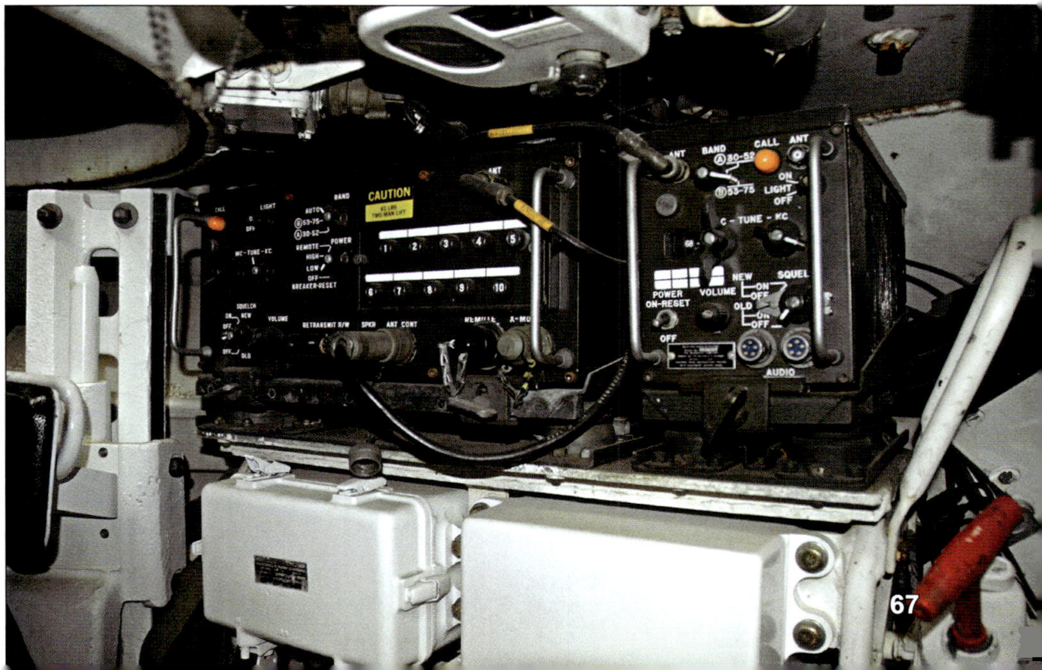

Below the radio, from left to right, are the amplifier integrator assembly and power supply assembly. A portable fire extinguisher is mounted in a bracket below the power supply assembly.

A second dome light is mounted on the ceiling in front of the radio set. The black knob on the right side of the light is its dimmer switch. The lever on the unit itself powers the light on and is used to select red or white light. It also acts as a safety to prevent the light from being turned on when the hatch is opened up.

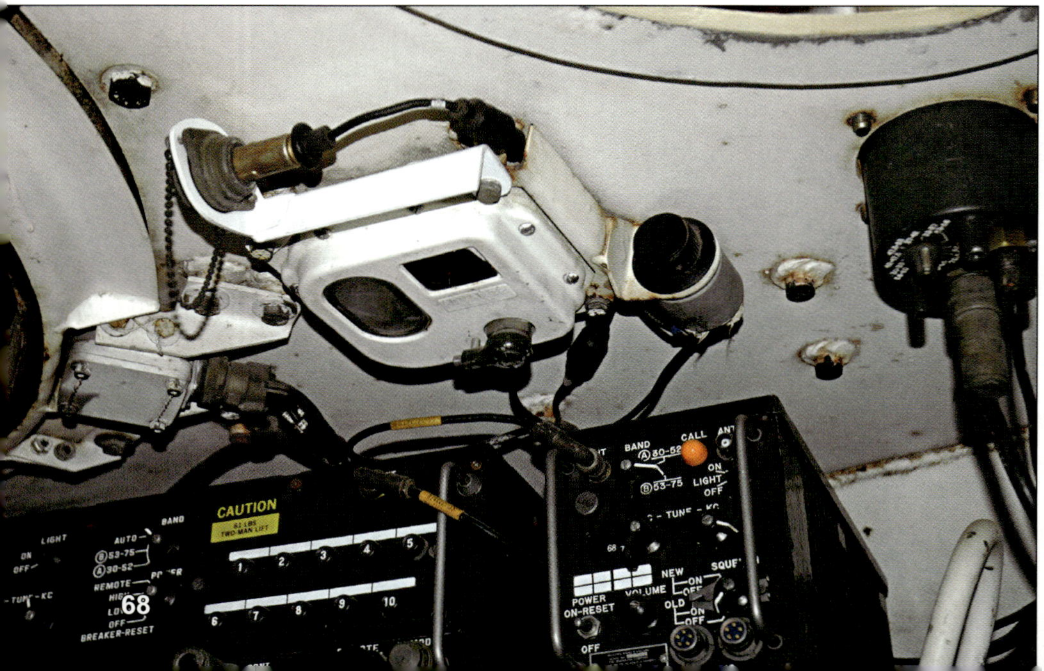

The antenna matching unit MX-2799/VRC plugs into the ceiling behind the loader's hatch opening. A switch on it automatically sets the appropriate frequency range for the antenna when the frequency is changed on the radio.

When closed, the loader's hatch cover is secured by sliding the handle towards the edge of the cover and then pushing it down into the slot on the locking bracket. The interior side of the hatch cover is painted the same as the vehicle exterior to maintain camouflage continuity with the rest of the exterior.

Vehicles equipped with the CBSS had a second air cylinder placed between the loader and commander's positions. It took the place of one of the vertical missile stowage racks. A fire extinguisher is here placed in the rack normally reserved for a missile.

Located on the turret floor near the rear CBSS air cylinder is the M8A3 gas-particulate filter system. A protective mask was provided for each crewmember with the hose being connected to the filter unit. This provided protection from poison gas.

Five 152mm rounds are held in the turret horizontal ammunition rack below the gun-launcher.

A second view of the turret horizontal ammunition racks also shows the bracket and pad that comprise the gunner's leg guard.

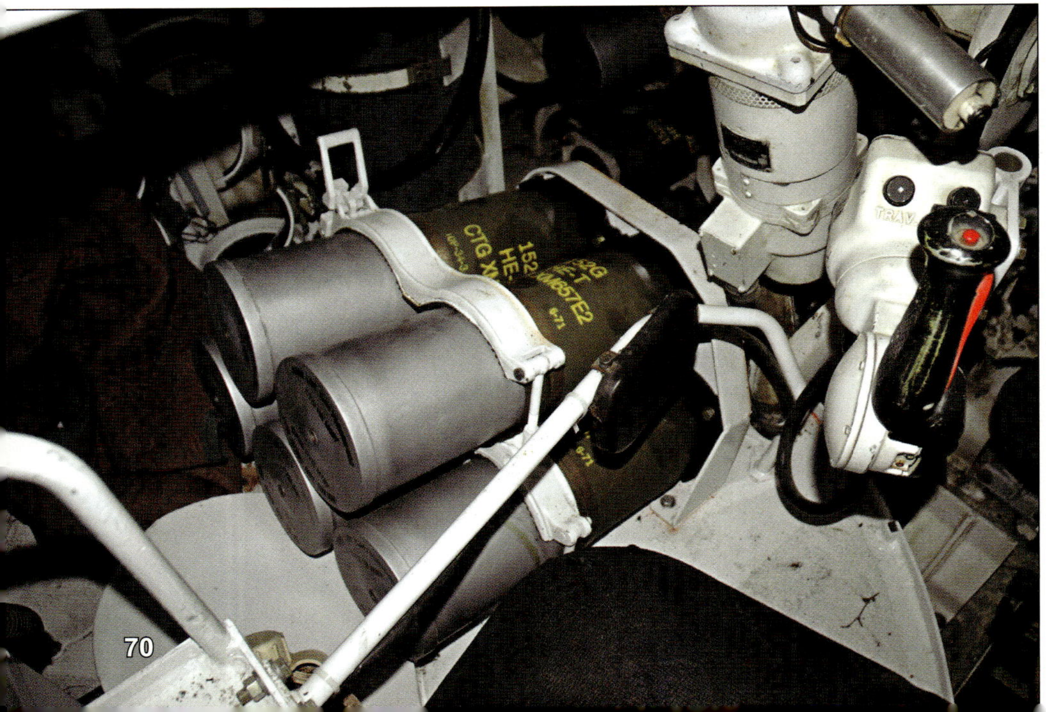

The driver sits in the front, center of the hull. The position of the seat back can be adjusted to provide proper support for the driver's back.

The position of the driver's seat is adjusted using the two levers on the seat support bracket. The lever on the left is the seat-positioning lever. On the right is the seat-adjusting lever.

A lever on the left, rear side of the seat allows the driver to flip the seat up and to the side in order to access the escape hatch.

The driver's escape-hatch cover is located below the driver's seat. In front of the seat and escape hatch is a torsion-bar cover.

The escape hatch is secured to the lower hull with a mounting bracket on one end and two plungers operated by a lever on the other end. When the lever is pulled towards the rear of the tank, the plungers are disengaged and the hatch falls to the ground.

Steering the M551 on land is accomplished using the land steer control or "T" bar located in front of the driver. A "T" shaped brake lock handle is mounted below the steer control bar. Behind the "T" bar is the driver's switch panel.

The driver's gearshift quadrant is located on the right side of the driver's compartment. The M551 has four forward gear ranges and two reverse ones. In front of the gear shift quadrant is the water steer knob.

The driver's indicator panel is located behind the left steering bard. It includes an odometer at the top, a tachometer/speedometer in the center, engine coolant temperature gauge on the left and a fuel gauge on the right.

Located behind the right steering bar is the driver's switch panel. Among the things on the panel are the engine starter switch, front and rear bilge pump switches, and the light switch assembly.

The driver's foot pedals are below the steer bar. In the center is the brake pedal with the accelerator pedal located to the right of it. The headlight dimmer switch is located to the left of the pedal. An angle headed flashlight is stored in a bracket to the left of the dimmer switch.

Attached to the ceiling to the left side of the driver is the slave cable receptacle used when slave starting the tank. Since the receptacle was located directly over the left side 152mm ammunition racks, electrical arcs during the slave process could cause ammunition fires. During the PIP instituted in 1977, the receptacle was moved to an external position on the glacis plate of many vehicles.

Located just behind the driver's left shoulder is one of the interior fire-extinguisher actuating handles and the fuel shut-off control handle. The fuel shut-off handle is in white and on the right. The cover of the fire-extinguisher actuating handle has been flipped up to expose the handle itself. Mounted on the ceiling above is a stowed M25A1 tank protective mask.

Mounted on the right side of the driver's compartment ceiling is the control box for the vehicle personnel heater. A high/low toggle switch is on the left, while the power toggle switch is on the right. To the right of the control box is the driver's compartment dome light.

The vehicle personnel heater is located in the right side of the driver's compartment, in front of and to the right of the ammunition racks. When not functioning properly, carbon monoxide fumes emitted by the heater could gas the vehicle crew.

With the hatch cover closed, the driver is restricted to using three M47 periscopes to view the outside. One of the periscopes is seen here in the center of the hatch.

When the driver's hatch is open, it rotates into the driver's compartment behind the driver's head. It is seen here from the loader's position.

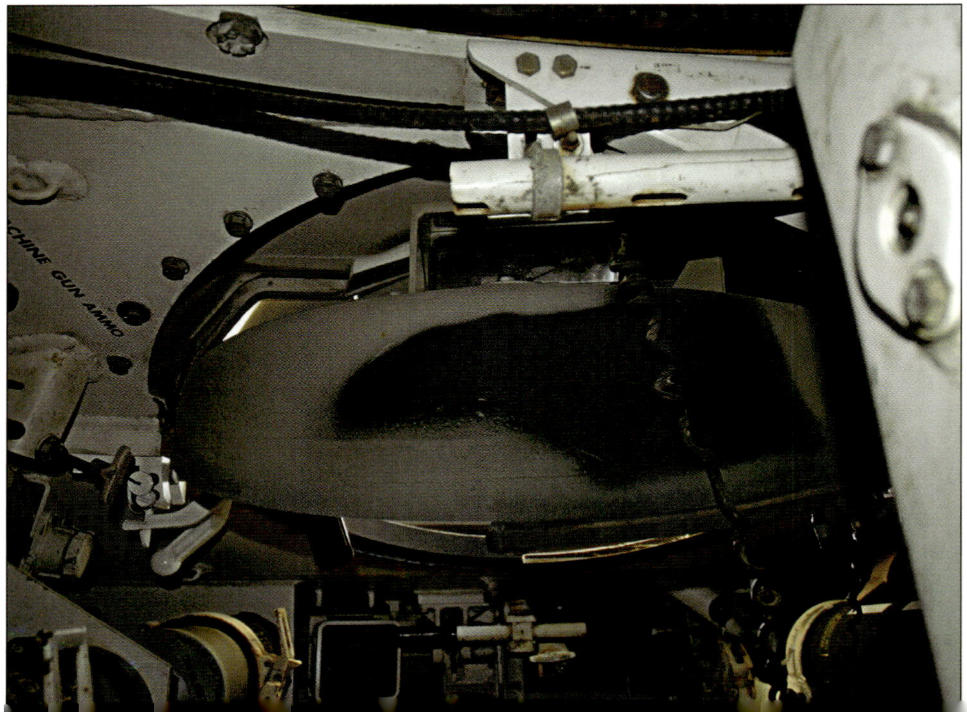

The rotatable driver's hatch cover is opened and closed using a locking handle mounted on the right front of the driver's compartment.

A periscope washer liquid reservoir and periscope washer pump are located on the left side of the driver's hatch cover. Because the hatch cover is open, the reservoir appears to be on the right side of the cover.

Ammunition for the 152mm gun-launcher is stored on both sides of the driver. Racks on the right side normally hold seven missiles but could hold conventional rounds.

A series of hinged arms hold the rounds in the racks until they are needed. The clamps are opened by pulling down on the locking lever, which in turn releases a "T" shaped catch at the bottom of the arm.

Two racks on the left side of the driver hold 13 conventional rounds. When equipped with the CBSS, 29 rounds of main gun ammunition are carried.

Seven conventional rounds are held in the left, front rack next to the driver. The combustible case cartridges are a silver-gray color.

Six more conventional rounds are stored in the left, rear ammunition rack. The rounds stored here are XM657E2 High Explosive Anti-Tank (HEAT) rounds.

A bin located behind the driver's seat stores the M48 infrared periscope. The M48 periscope is used in conjunction with infrared driving lights.

The crew compartment bilge pump is located in the front of the left hand side ammunition racks. It pumped water out of the crew compartment during amphibious operations.

A pair of 200-round ammunition boxes for the co-axial 7.62mm machine gun are stored between the driver's seat and the M48 periscope box.

Ten torsion bars run the width of the hull floor of the M551, with each torsion bar connecting to its corresponding road-wheel station. The orange hose above the torsion bars is the personnel-heater duct.

An additional 200-round ammunition box is stored in a bracket on the right hand side of the hull floor in front of the turret basket. In the foreground, bolted to the hull floor, a pad supports the rear of a missile stored in the right hand side ammunition rack.

M551 Sheridan Development

Prototype XM551

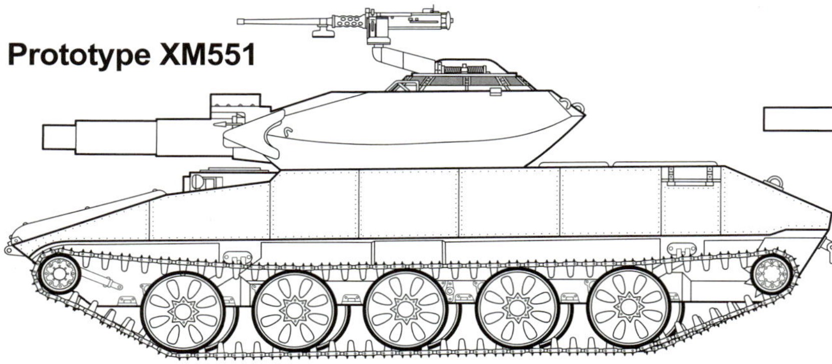

Sheridan/T-72 (OPFOR)

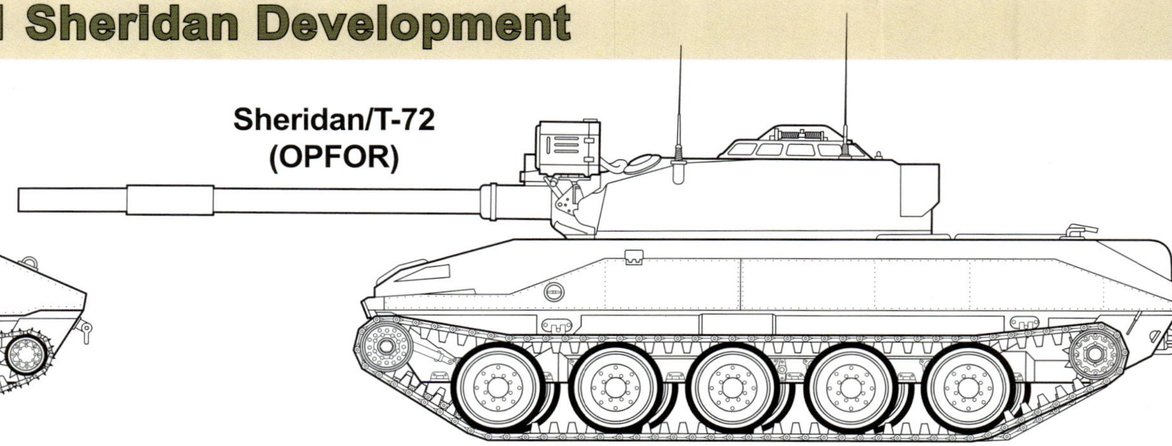

M551 (Early)

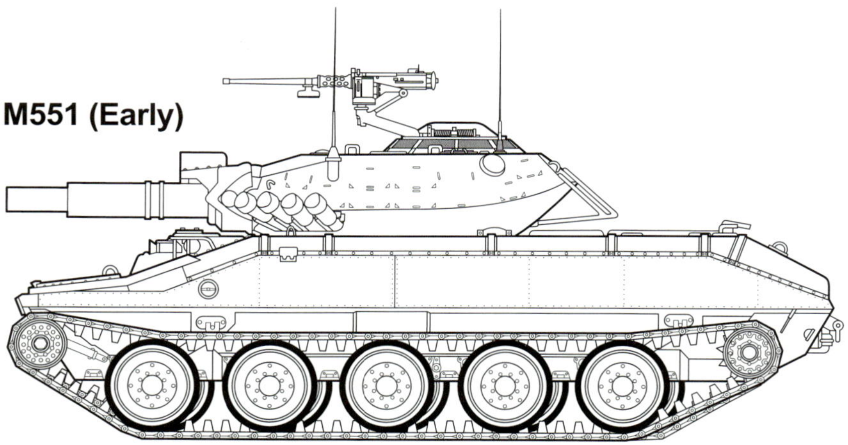

Sheridan/BMP (OPFOR)

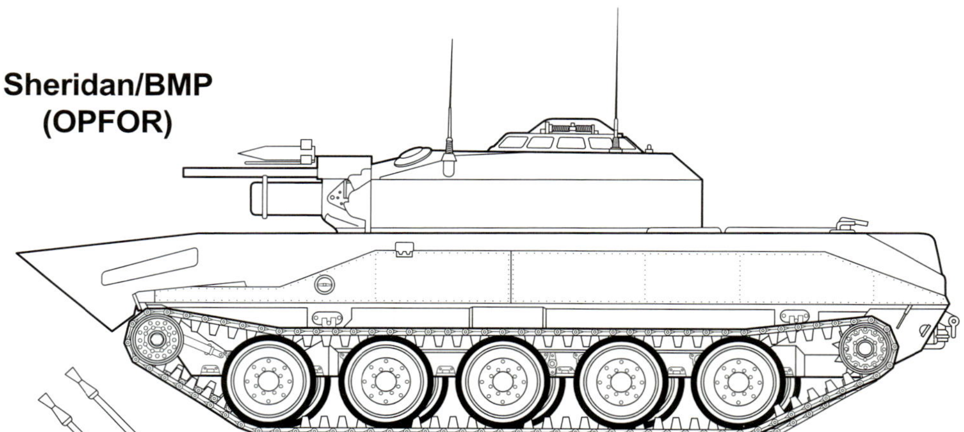

M551A1

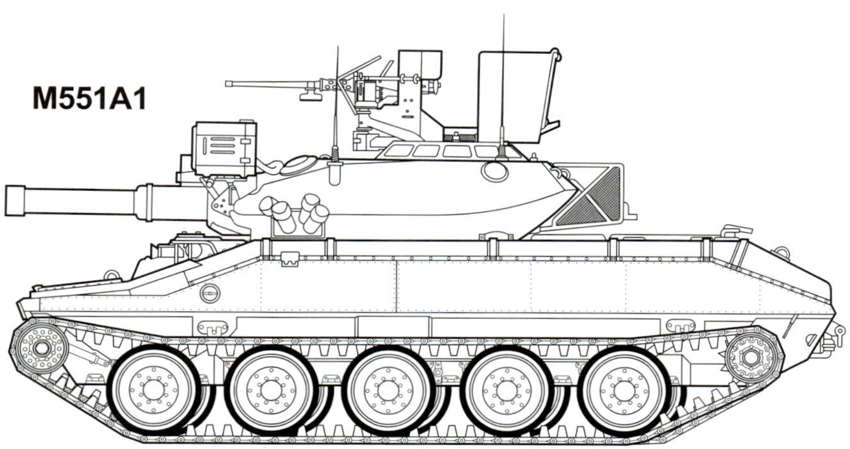

Sheridan/ ZSU-23-4 (OPFOR)

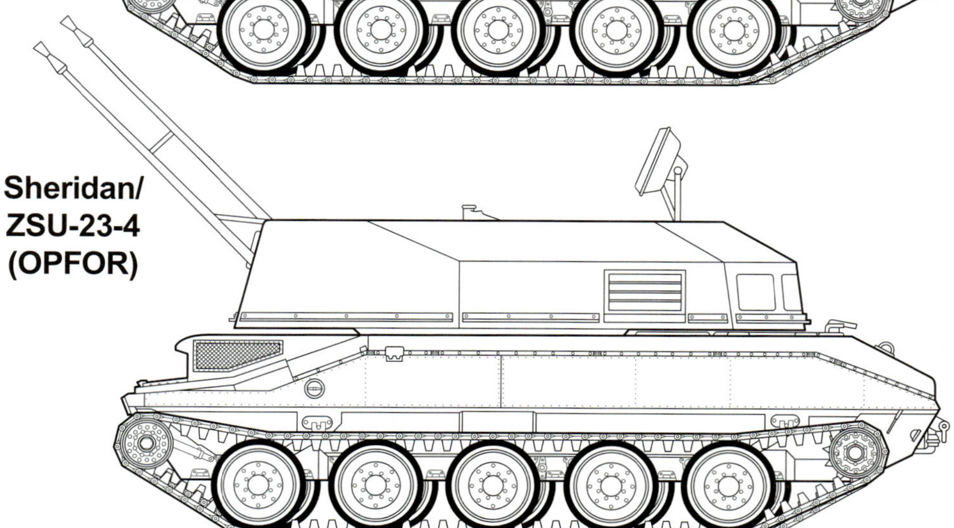

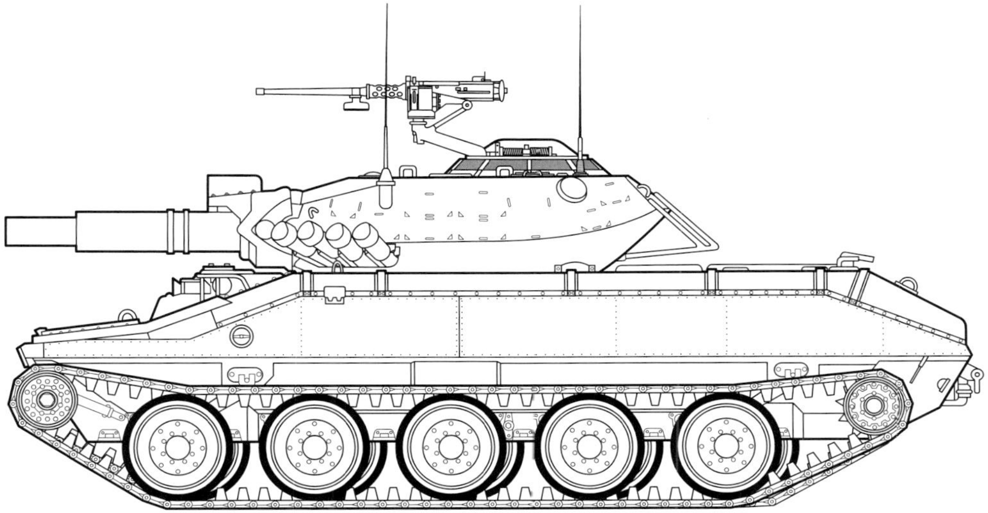

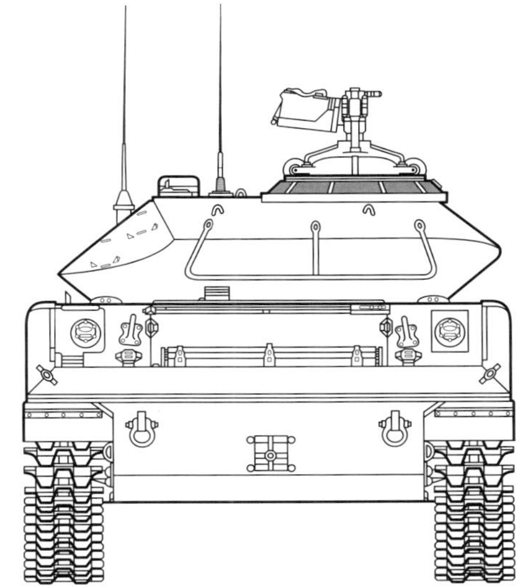

Specifications

M551 Sheridan

Crew........................Four
Length....................20.43 Feet
Width......................9.25 Feet
Height.....................9.66 Feet
Weight....................34,899 Pounds

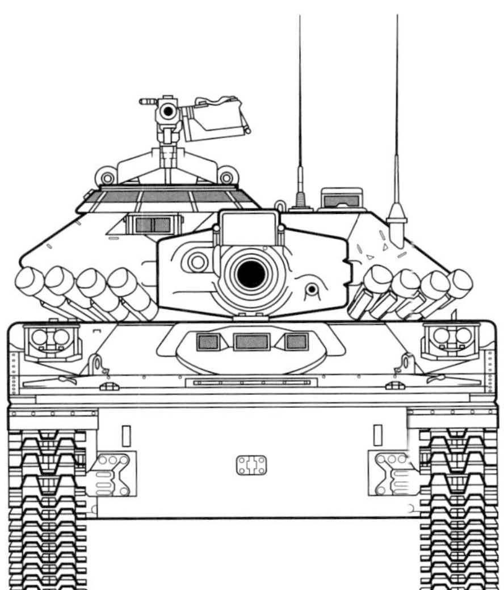

Armament

Main.........................152mm gun/missile launcher

Secondary...............One 7.62mm coaxial machine gun, one .50-caliber M2 Browning on commander's cupola

Engine......................Detroit-Diesel 6V-53T 300 h.p. turbocharged diesel engine

Speed........................43.5 m.p.h.

Range........................373 miles

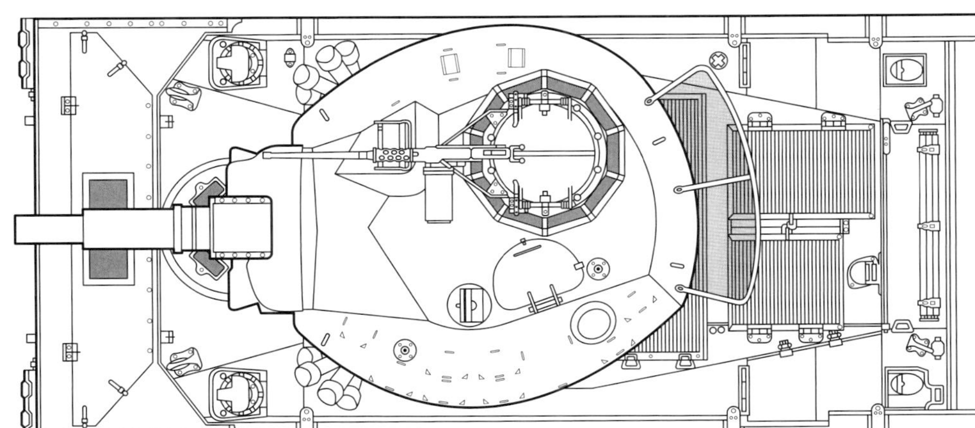

In spite of many technical and mechanical issues, the M551 Sheridan served in the U.S. Army in one shape or form for over 35 years. It has been the only air-droppable tank to see service with the Army and as of this writing; a replacement for it has yet to be procured.